D0955432

CONTENTS

Photography: Ron Reagan, front and back endpapers, frontis, 6, 10 bottom, 11, 12, 13, 14, 32, 60, 79, 86, 88, 90, 91, 92, 93, 94, 95, 100, 101, 103, 105, 107, 110, 111, 112, 113, 114, 115, 116, 118, 120, 122, 123. Paul Stankus (courtesy of Ruth Zimmermann), 104. Ruth Zimmermann, 81, 82, 83, 84, 85, 108, 124.

Frontis: Kadette's Puncherino of Dei-jai, Blue Point male. Breeder, Patricia G. Goodbold. Owner, Doris Thoms.

To Mom and Dad

ISBN 0-87666-860-0

Distributed in the UNITED STATES by T.F.H. Publications, Inc., 211 West Sylvania Avenue, Neptune City, NJ 07753; in CANADA by H & L Pet Supplies Inc., 27 Kingston Crescent, Kitchener, Ontario N2B 2T6; Rolf C. Hagen Ltd., 3225 Sartelon Street, Montreal 382 Quebec; in ENGLAND by T.F.H. Publications Limited, 4 Kier Park, Ascot, Berkshire SL5 7DS; in AUSTRALIA AND THE SOUTH PACIFIC by T.F.H. (Australia) Pty. Ltd., Box 149, Brookvale 2100 N.S.W., Australia; in NEW ZEALAND by Ross Haines & Son, Ltd., 18 Monmouth Street, Grey Lynn, Auckland 2 New Zealand; in SINGAPORE AND MALAYSIA by MPH Distributors Pte., 71-77 Stamford Road, Singapore 0617; in the PHILIPPINES by Bio-Research, 5 Lippay Street, San Lorenzo Village, Makati, Rizal; in SOUTH AFRICA by Multipet Pty. Ltd., 30 Turners Avenue, Durban 4001. Published by T.F.H. Publications Inc., Ltd., the British Crown Colony of Hong Kong.

SIAMESE
CATS

RON REAGAN

Above: Ch. Nicholas Jay of Rocat, one-year-old Seal Point male by Mardi's Quasar of Fefe x Ch. Dei-jai's Tabatha of Fefe. Breeder, Laurie L. Sarno. Owner, Catherine Rowan. **Facing page:** Four kittens that display the various "points," i.e., ear, face, tail, and foot color.

ACKNOWLEDGMENTS

I am so grateful to the many people who gave so generously of their time, assistance, patience, understanding and encouragement. Cathy Rowan (Rocat Cattery, Trenton, New Jersey) put up with me on many different occasions while I photographed her lovely cats and kittens who appear so frequently on these pages. Bill and Doris Thoms (Dei-Jai Cattery, Hackettstown, New Jersey) twice welcomed me into their home to photograph their cats and kittens. To Janice Lees, Susan P. Tilton, the W.T. Reichles, A. Louise Zimmer-Vafiadis and Barbara and Donald Dulberg thank you too for letting me into your homes. A big thank you to Ruth Zimmermann for the excellent photos of your Siamese queen giving birth. Thank yous also to Natalie del Vecchio and the folks at The Photo Center, Bricktown, New Jersey. Phyllis Lauder, thank you for inspiration you didn't know you gave. And of course, for their incessant comments, I must acknowledge the "help" given by Meow, Poodie, the Pumpkin, the Baby, Choochie, Brownie, Ingrid and the Munchkin.

Author's Foreword

I hope this little book helps to introduce new or potential cat owners and fanciers to the wonderful Siamese, a most delightful companion. There is no detailed breed history here, because I think such a history would more properly belong to a much larger and more comprehensive volume. I have tried to cover things that you, the responsible cat owner, should know about the day-to-day care of your new feline friend. Additionally, I have included a section on first aid that I hope you will never need but, in case you ever do, you will find information which will enable you to help your cat or even save its life.

Cats are becoming increasingly more popular as more people realize what a joy they are to have around. Contrary to stories often heard, cats are not by nature aloof, anti-social or sinister. When you get your new pet, handle and talk to it frequently. Soon your new housemate will overcome the initial fear of its new surroundings; it will return your attention and affection and will make your home its own domain. The cat owner has to keep in mind that cats do not relate to us as dogs do but as cats do, and they are every bit as affectionate. Ask any cat owner about the head-bonk, the nose-nip, the chirp or the newspaper sit and you will learn something of the happiness of owning a cat.

If you do intend to bring a cat into your life, please be responsible and learn beforehand what keeping a cat entails. Take the time to learn what kinds of cats are available to you so that you can choose what you truly want. There are far too many abandoned cats in our shelters because people didn't care.

I wish you and your new cat long lives filled with health and happiness.

· **Facing page, above:** A queen carries her kit to safety. **Below:** Ch. Suzzi's Rembrandt of Velvet Paws, eight-year-old Chocolate Point male. by Ch. Suzzi's Count Dragula x Suzzi's Never On Sunday. Breeders, Mr. and Mrs. William A. Ramsden, Jr. Owners, Doris and Bill Thoms. **Above:** The coloring on this six-week-old Chocolate Point kitten is coming in very well and may promise a bright show career. Breeders, Doris and Bill Thoms.

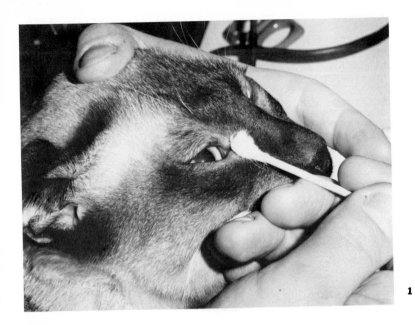

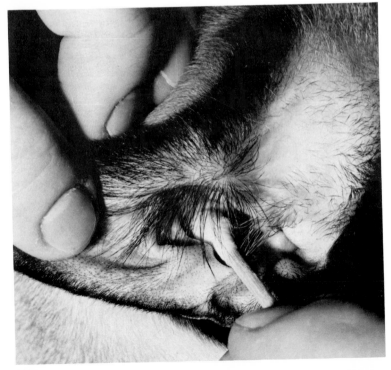

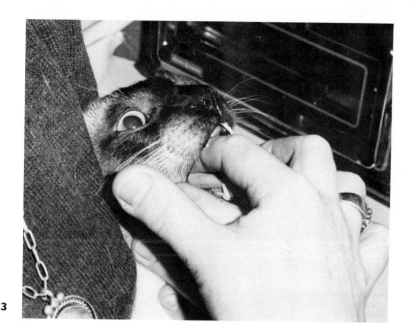

3

Up to here a few pretty pictures and thoughts of how much fun it would be to have a cat. You're absolutely right, you'd love it. But hold on a moment—are you willing to be a responsible cat owner? Will you clean your pet's eyes and ears when they need it? And how about when your cat's sick? Will you take it to the vet and then faithfully administer whatever medications are necessary or will you take the position that after a few days of rest all will be well? All of a sudden owning a cat doesn't appeal to you? Fine; read on, enjoy the pictures and whenever you want to play with a cat visit a friend who has one—both you and any cat you might have owned will be much happier and better off.

1. When cleaning your cat's eyes be gentle and of course don't go poking into the eye. You can use a cotton swab as indicated or a wetted piece of paper towel or hankie, but please stay away from scented tissue or toilet paper as the scenting agent may bother your pet's eyes. 2. Cleaning your pet's ears regularly will help to prevent any wax build-up from accumulating there. Never probe too deeply into the ear canal and don't use a dirty swab on your pet. Don't take the attitude that it's o.k. to use the same swab in your cat's ear that you used to lubricate a part on your sewing machine. 3. Giving a cat a pill. Photos by the author.

Facing page: A.M.P. Kara Grace of Rocat, Seal Tortie Point Siamese/Seal Tortie Colorpoint Shorthair by Altair's Mickey of A.M.P. x Dbl. Ch. A.M.P. Queen Lizz. Breeder, Anna M. Pauch. Owner, Catherine Rowan. **Above:** Active breeds like the Siamese can be let outdoors for fresh air, sunshine, and exercise, provided they are supervised at all times in an enclosed area.

This book is so valuable to anyone who doesn't really know what breed of cat he or she would most like. All of the breeds recognized here in the U.S. are discussed and there are many photos to illustrate the different varieties available. If you are undecided, this is a very good place to start looking.

To The Prospective Cat Owner

WHICH BREED IS FOR YOU?

A prospective cat owner usually decides between a pure-bred or non-purebred cat. The second decision is usually a choice between a shorthaired or longhaired breed (most new cat fanciers are not yet aware of the third variety, the rex-coated breeds). From this point on, the selection process becomes more difficult.

Unless one has read a lot of cat books with a large number of photos, attended many cat shows with a large number of breeds exhibited or has a large number of friends who own many different breeds of cats, he likely knows very little about the various cat breeds and their color varieties. If he needs to know all the options open to him before making a decision, he will probably not be able to buy a cat until satisfied that he has learned just what is available. He should get a good comprehensive book all about cats such as Meredith Wilson's "Encyclopedia Of American Cat Breeds." Any breed accepted by at least one of the various U.S. registering associations is covered in this useful volume. He should read the descriptions of the various breeds and study the pictures. In this way he will at least be able to select several, if not just the right one, of the breeds he is most attracted to. His next step is to attend a cat show and actually see live animals. He should not be disappointed if he is not allowed to touch very many of the cats on exhibit. Many exhibitors do not allow their cats to be handled at shows because this is an easy way to spread germs among cats from different catteries. After a few shows, however, he should be able to determine further which is the right breed for him. Additionally, he will have met breeders of the cats he is interested in and will have been able to have made appointments to visit their catteries.

Before this last step is taken, however, several more questions have to be answered before one buys his perfect pet.

KITTEN OR CAT?

There is certainly a great amount of appeal in raising a kitten, but the fascination of kittenhood does not last over that long a period of time. A new kitten will require more human attention than a new adult will and someone in the family will have to be responsible for the kitten's care. There will likely be cleaning up after the kitten to be done, at least for the first few days, until the little one becomes accustomed to its new surroundings. One advantage in purchasing a kitten rather than an adult is the fact that it is so impressionable when young and, therefore, very receptive to your own personality and temperament. A mature cat is likely to be rather set in its ways. An advantage in acquiring an older cat that you feel comfortable with is that its mien is not likely to change whereas you can never be sure just how a kitten will develop in spite of the influences it receives.

Many prospective cat owners do not feel that they have the time, or choose not to take the time, to work with a kitten. For such persons a ready-made pet, a mature cat of good disposition, is their best choice. Persons with the desire and time to spend playing with, training and just being with a kitten will enjoy the experience of raising a youngster to the fullest and will probably be happiest if they buy a kitten rather than an adult. An elderly person may not be able to take care of a kitten, but a trained, affectionate adult is the perfect pet for such a person. It will give him or her affection, attention and companionship, will require very little money to maintain and will provide endless hours of amusement and pleasure.

The family with a dog would do best to buy a kitten since an adult cat often does not easily take to a dog, views it as a pest and often resents it, even when the dog was living in the home first. A kitten, however, readily accepts a dog as a playmate, a warm bed, a confidant and a friend. Unless of bad temperament, a dog usually accepts a cat as a source of fun and play if nothing else, and often as a member of the family to be cared for, loved and protected. Puppies and kittens invariably become fast friends, especially when they are brought into a home at the same time.

Families with children have to choose carefully whether or not to buy a feline. They should decide whether a non-feline pet might be a better choice for their household. Cats do not like to be rough-housed, and if the family's children are too young to respect a cat, particularly its need for privacy occasionally, its right to choose when and when not to play, its right not to be handled like a dog and its warning growls and postures, the family should not acquire a cat. Cats are capable of inflicting serious injuries to a child, and while such actions are invariably retaliatory in nature, parents will probably blame the cat for their child's misbehavior. When children have grown up with cats and the family wants to replace a cat that has died, there should be no problem in reaching a decision to purchase another. If the first cat and the children had gotten along in the past, a new cat will be welcomed; if not, a non-feline pet should be considered if the family is set on bringing a new pet into the home.

MALE OR FEMALE?

Unless you intend to later breed your cat and need one sex rather than the other, the sex of the kitten you buy doesn't matter. You have doubtless heard various cat owners claim that their males are more affectionate than their females or vice versa, or that one sex is more intelligent than the other or similar remarks. If you were to tabulate these claims you would probably find a 50-50 split among them.

As a responsible cat owner you should have your pet neutered (altered, "fixed"). This will end your cat's sex drives and accompanying habits. A neutered female is called a spay, a neutered male an alter or castrate. The spay will no longer go into heat cycles or cry for a mate, and the neighborhood toms will no longer be at your door spraying and trying to mate your female. She will also be spared from having cysts develop on her ovaries if she is not bred. Your alter will no longer strive to get out of the house at every opportunity and will not get into serious fights with other males should he encounter them. Both sexes will become most content to remain at home, and it does seem to be true that neuters become more people-oriented. If the diet of a neuter is regulated, and if it receives enough exercise and opportunity to play, there is no reason why it should become fat. If you notice that your cat is overweight, reduce its food ration until it regains its condition. Just remember to continue to feed a balanced diet. The quality of the diet remains the same, only the quantity is reduced.

The cat's doctor will advise you when your pet is old enough to be neutered. Normally you will bring your cat to the surgery early in the morning. A male can usually be brought home that same afternoon, but because the surgical procedure on a female is more complicated, she often spends the night at the hospital and is not brought home until the following day. This may vary with individual cats and veterinarians. Your vet will tell you what kind of after-care is required for your cat.

PET, BREEDER OR SHOW?

A pet cat is just that—a pet. Nothing more than companionship is expected from it. For whatever reasons, a pet quality cat does not conform to the ideal breed standard (which is drawn up and regularly revised by experts in the fancy). Often only the most experienced cat fancier is able to detect what a pet quality cat's shortcomings are.

A breeder is a cat of superior quality used to produce kittens. The responsible owner does not breed his females more than three times every two years. A stud male can service many females in a year, but he should be regularly rested and allowed to rejuvenate himself.

Show cats are those considered by an owner to be his best representatives of the ideal breed standard. If regularly shown these cats require extensive care and grooming, and, therefore, a lot of their owner's time. Many stud males are also show cats, but most of the females being shown are not bred during their show career as breeding obviously makes excessive demands on the tip-top condition required of a show cat.

So, what have I said? Nothing more than to explain what the terms pet, breeder and show mean when used within the cat fancy. As a prospective cat owner you are most interested in acquiring a healthy cat of a chosen breed, possibly of a particular sex or age, and probably of a certain color or colors. If you have carefully chosen what you wanted and waited until such was available, you are almost guaranteed a most enjoyable and lasting relationship with a wonderful animal. Whether you chose to buy a pet, breeder or show cat, treat it as a pet. Loving contact between our cat and ourselves enhances the relationship between us. It contributes to the cat's well-being and temperament while increasing our enjoyment, understanding and appreciation of our cats at the same time.

WHERE TO FIND WHAT YOU WANT

If you are looking for a pet, a cat you do not intend to breed or show, you have numerous sources. Veterinarians often know which of their clients have animals available. Some petshops sell felines, and a responsible dealer backs up each sale with a health guarantee. If you buy from such a dealer, he will be able to supply you with pet accessories and will often stock the special diets carried only in pet-shops. Responsible pet stores are interested in your future business and make every attempt to secure it by dealing with you responsibly.

Quality breeder or show cats can only be purchased from people who carefully and responsibly breed cats. The large cat associations have breed clubs affiliated with them, and the people there can direct you to the appropriate club. The breed club will then refer you to reputable breeders in your area. Another way to locate a breeder is by attending a cat show. As you admire the cats you will be able to meet and talk with their breeders. There is a strong possibility that any cat you meet at a show is either father, mother, brother or sister to a kitten that you might purchase. This is important for reasons that will be discussed later.

The "Cats Classified" section of *Cats Magazine* is still another valuable source for the prospective cat owner. It lists, alphabetically by breed, catteries throughout the U.S. and Canada. The individual breed entries are arranged geographically, and this makes it very easy for you to locate breeders nearby to your home.

HOW MUCH TO PAY

The price range for cats is broad indeed. A proven adult show animal may cost from $400 to $1000 or more as can a quality breeder of demonstrated ability. A pet kitten usually costs up to about $200. Kittens from championship lines often cost up to $500, but this depends on their individual quality more than that of their parents. An experienced breeder knows how his stock develops, and his opinion of a kitten's potential should carry much weight with a prospective buyer. Often a breeder will lower his price on a kitten if the buyer intends to show it since such exposure advances the breeder's cattery and line. If you purchase a kitten under such an agreement you owe it to the breeder to follow through on your promise. The same moral obligation is owed the seller should you purchase a kitten for further breeding. Most breeders are cooperative when they believe buyers are serious about these matters. A breeder may arrange a time payment plan with the buyer of an expensive kitten or cat; this will often be set down in the form of a written agreement. A reputable breeder stands behind his animals, and should a drastic health complication develop despite all efforts to prevent it, an adjustment will usually be made.

Prices vary according to breed, color and sex. In some areas certain breeds are more readily available than others and therefore less expensive than they would be in an area where the breed is not widely bred. Additionally, some breeds are more expensive than others simply because they are more popular.

As a prospective buyer you might question the price asked for a kitten or cat. Cats are not inexpensive to breed and it takes years of learning to successfully become a good breeder. You are paying for the breeder's knowledge and competency as well as for the cat itself. Many people feel that if they pay well for something, whether a refrigerator, dress, home, pet or whatever, they will then take care of it properly. While this may not always hold true, the vast majority of us who are not wealthy tend to value something we pay dearly for. The old saying "You get what you pay for" is very often applicable when purchasing a purebred cat. Finally, when you consider that you are buying something that will last for a long time, you are not really spending very much for something that will bring you so much joy and happiness over so long a period of time.

WAITING FOR THE RIGHT CAT

After you have carefully considered the breed, color and sex of the cat you would like to have you are ready to buy it. Don't purchase the first animal that catches your eye unless it is truly just what you are looking for. All kittens are appealing and attractive, but because they vary in appearance and personality as adults you should buy with this fact in mind. You may have to wait for a cat of the color or sex that you want, but you will not become disenchanted later if you wait for what you really prefer.

Remember that your pet will live with you for many years. Don't buy one cat with the intention of keeping it only until a cat of the exact type you want becomes available.

BEFORE YOU BUY

First you decided that you wanted a cat and chose in your mind the breed you wanted. Next you decided on color and sex, whether you wanted an adult or kitten, and whether you wanted a pet, breeder or show animal. You located a breeder and may even have seen a kitten or cat to your liking. Are you now ready to purchase it? Emphatically not.

Cats, like people, are a product of both their genetics and their environment. I mentioned earlier that it is a good idea to see a kitten's parents before purchasing a kitten. This will enable you to judge the adults' temperaments. If you neither like nor feel comfortable with them, you may well have doubts about their offspring. Allowance must be made for the fact that many cats do not like to receive visitors, and this is especially true of a queen with a young litter. Cats, however, should not be overly skittish or nervous, and should certainly not be aggressive toward strangers welcomed into the home by the cats' owners. Because kittens are influenced by the people around them, you should feel comfortable with their owners. If these are not the type of people with which you would associate, you might not appreciate the influence they have had on the kittens. Remember to check the kitten for fleas, ear mites and the like, get a complete medical history of the kitten and a list of its diet up to the time of purchase. Of course you won't forget its papers if you are buying a purebred will you?

Common Sense Cat Care

CHOOSING A VET

If you already own a cat you surely have a family veterinarian. But if you have recently moved or have become a pet owner for the first time you will need to find a vet. A particular veterinary doctor is often suggested to you by the breeder from whom you purchased your pet. You may choose a vet from the yellow pages and select one close to your home, or you may hear of one by reputation. Perhaps a friend will recommend one to you. However you select him, a veterinarian should be decided on early. If you are comfortable with him and respect him it is a good idea to stick with him for the life of your cat just as you do with your own personal physician. This is helpful to both of you as the doctor will thoroughly know your cat's personal health history and you will have someone you can count on as regards your pet's health.

You yourself should not play doctor; your general knowledge of symptoms aids your vet in treating your cat and could be especially valuable in case of a true emergency situation, but it is not enough to enable you to substitute for experienced veterinary care. The more you do know about cat care the better, but be sure that what you learn is from reliable sources and is accurate. Incorrect treatment is as injurious as the ailment treated in many cases. Knowing what to do when your cat is in shock, poisoned, shot, hit by a car or something else similarly serious enables you to properly care for your pet until the doctor comes; in many cases what you know is what will make the difference between your cat's surviving or dying. Remember that you are supplementing and not supplanting veterinary care; learn all you can about day to day care of your pet and what is needed to keep it healthy. If illness strikes, your recognition of symptoms as they develop will aid your vet in prescribing the proper medications.

KEEPING RECORDS

You should maintain a records file for your cat in which you keep registration papers, dates and results of immunizations, wormings and tests, dates booster shots are due and any other medical or breeding information. This system makes it very easy for you to find information whenever needed and helps you to know when regular veterinary care and treatment are due.

While not pleasant to think about, if you should die, the person or persons to whom you have left your cats will know how to care for them. You can indicate in each cat's file its food preferences, its allergies and other useful data that you normally carry around in your head. For obvious reasons your pet's shot record should be kept up to date. All of us have many things to think about; when things are written down they are less easily ignored or forgotten.

FEEDING

Cats should be fed a balanced diet high in protein. Many of the commercially prepared cat foods are complete in themselves; their base is fish, fowl, beef or organ meats to which vitamin and mineral supplements and cereal have been added. Not all canned or boxed cat foods are complete foods, however, and you will have to read the label to find out which are. Government regulation of the pet food industry is quite strict, and only those that meet all of the cat's nutritional requirements may indicate this on their labels.

You will find that your cat enjoys a varied diet. Ideally, dry food or kibbles, canned food and people food should be offered. Most canned foods are complete and should be served once a day. Dry kibbles are often a favorite item in the feline diet and help to keep the cat's teeth free from tar-

tar. Table scraps can also be fed, and you will be surprised at what your pet will eat if offered. You must be very careful not to feed chicken or fish bones which easily splinter and can quite easily become stuck in your pet's throat. Some of the people foods that cats usually favor include egg yolk, egg salad, cottage cheese, milk, cheese, liver, kidney, chicken, raw ground meat and unsugared breakfast cereals that crunch a lot. You may notice that your cat loves milk but gets diarrhea from it. Try giving powdered milk instead of fresh milk and diarrhea may no longer be a problem.

Fresh food should not be allowed to lie about for long as bacteria such as salmonella could grow there. Never leave wet food for your cats when you go on a trip, but only dry kibbles. Flies will lay their eggs in the moist food and after several days these eggs will have become maggots.

Occasionally your cat will "go off" its food. Usually this is nothing to worry about and after a day or two it will be eating normally. Your cat may have eaten a fly, cockroach or something similar and gotten sick from bug spray that may have been on or in the pest. Another possibility is that your pet has tired of particular foods. Change its diet a bit; try other brands and varieties. You might keep a list of what your cat likes and dislikes. Some cats eat dog food, but the large-chunk varieties are too big for most cats to swallow. If your cat does like a dog food, offer it once in a while as a treat. Remember that a cat's dietary requirements are different from a dog's, and what is a complete food for a dog is not necessarily so for your cat. It is quite often the case that on hot summer days cats eat less than usual. This is normal feline behavior and is to be expected.

Feeding should be at regular times. If you feed your cat twice a day, then morning and evening feeding is best as it coincides with your meals. Kibbles can be left out as a snack. Water must be available at all times and should be changed frequently. Some people provide a communal feeding dish for their cats; others feel that each pet should have its own dish. Some cats are gulpers, others are pickers and still others are slow but deliberate eaters. An individual dish allows each cat to eat at its own pace comfortably. Cats eat until they are full even if this means leaving food in the dish. New cat owners who were formerly dog owners are often surprised by this as dogs eat until there's nothing left in the bowl. Although you may notice that your cats change dishes with each other when eating, each will get its proper share of the food if enough has been provided. There are differing opinions as to how much is the right amount to feed. After your cat is full grown feed it enough to maintain

Most pet shops carry a wide variety of products designed to be of value to cat owners. Ask your dealer and your cat-owning friends about what products they recommend.

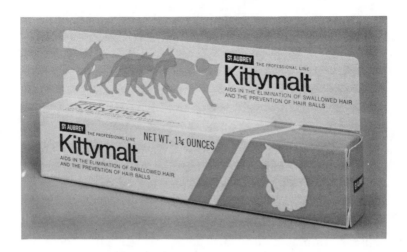

Hairballs are a problem, especially in warmer weather, and even when you regularly brush your cat (which is of course the recommended course of action), hairballs will still form when your cat grooms itself. A number of products on the market are effective against hairballs.

its condition, weight and appetite. If your pet becomes overweight, lessen the amount of food offered. Before your cat is full grown, allow it to eat as much as it wants so that its skeleton and muscles develop properly. If your young cat eats an obviously overmuch amount of food for its size worms are to be expected and a fecal sample should be taken to your vet for analysis.

Some people salt their cat's food in summer to encourage it to drink more. Cats drink when they are thirsty, and it is not unreasonable to assume they drink more when they are hot. It seems quite unnecessary to salt their food. Extra moisture can always be added to their diet by feeding milk, eggnog, chicken broth or beef stock. Most cats relish some or all of these and gleefully accept them when offered.

The most important thing to remember about your cat's diet is that it should consist of complete, balanced foods fed regularly. If your cat cannot digest something it has eaten, it will probably vomit it right up. In this way you will learn what not to feed it. Each cat is an individual, and while some things such as chicken, liver and shrimp are enjoyed by most cats, yours may be one that turns away even from these items. Learn what your cat likes and vary its diet with these foods; they are sure to be found among the many complete and balanced varieties available.

INDOORS OR OUTDOORS?

Early on as a cat owner you will have to decide whether your cat will be kept as an indoor pet or be allowed to run free outdoors. The greatest dangers to cats other than infectious feline enteritis and pneumonitis are cars and large dogs. Because of the large numbers of these in cities and densely populated suburban areas, cats that live there are best kept indoors. Farm, ranch and country cats can easily be allowed to both roam freely and live in with the family. But what about the cat that lives in a small town or lightly populated suburb? If there are major roads nearby, it should not be allowed to run free. Additionally, if many of the neighborhood dogs are let to roam at large (which they shouldn't be permitted to do but often are) the small-town cat is best kept inside. When the neighborhood is rather peaceful, without many cars or dogs, cats can be let out but often at the expense of a neighbor's good will.

Unless your cat is a "mouser" that works on a farm, ranch or in the country, there seems to be no reason for it to be let loose outside. It may be that the only reason so many cats are seen running free is because their owners are not as responsible for their care as they could and should be.

There are several reasons against allowing a cat to run loose in addition to the dangers presented to it by cars and dogs. A free-running, attractive cat can easily be stolen. Since tattooing is not yet widely employed to identify them, stolen cats can easily be sold. There is also the possibility that a roaming cat will be picked up by the municipal animal patrol and brought to the pound. Many people do not take kindly to a cat that digs in their garden, annoys their pets or marks their house. A BB gun, or perhaps even a rifle or shotgun, may be waiting for the cat's next visit. Some people put out poison on their grounds to kill any animals that come there, and a free-running cat is also susceptible to secondary poisoning if it eats a contaminated mouse or rat. Road tar is another hazard to the outdoor cat, especially in the summer. The free-to-roam cat can get sick through exposure to lawn and tree sprays, lime or insecticides. Because of the large number of stray cats, it would not be unlikely for an outdoor cat to return home bearing the marks of a fight. Outdoor cats are likely to pick up fleas and ticks, may encounter a rabid animal and contract rabies or may have an unfortunate encounter with a skunk or porcupine. All of us cat owners have been repulsed by the actions of juveniles who have gotten their kicks by skinning, tar and feathering, drowning or in other ways torturing cats. Since cats often like to lie down beneath a parked car, we must be very careful when pulling out of the driveway.

Although opinions vary about this, it can be argued that a cat that lives outside most of the time will not be as affectionate and loving a companion as a housepet since it will want to roam around with its outdoor friends. Part of the reason for this has to be caused by its lack of frequent contact with people. This is also bound to affect the way one feels about the cat as well. When the cat ages, its owner will likely not feel the affection for it he would have had it spent its time with him during the preceding years. It may be quite possible that the owner won't care for it at all and the cat will lead a truly miserable life in its last years.

Some owners put their cats outside for the fresh air and sunshine but tie them up to restrict them. This is extremely dangerous if there are dogs about as the cat has no way to escape from the place it is tied. Even if no dogs are about, there is always the possibility that a cat tied up could strangle itself accidentally. There is, however, a single safe method of keeping a cat outdoors. This is through the use of an outdoor run such as those used at breeding or boarding catteries. Runs provide the cat with ample room to exercise and healthful exposure to the sun and air. Additionally, they protect the cat from unwelcome guests and prevent it from running into the road. Some runs are elaborately constructed and include year-round living quarters, but a sturdy, serviceable backyard exercise run can be easily built by the home handyman. A portable kennel for a large dog can be used as a cat exercise area for shorter periods of time.

The indoor cat, while not threatened by cars or dogs, encounters dangers of another sort as a result of its natural curiosity and our negligence. Common sense dictates that if we put down rat poison in our garage or cellar we don't allow our pets there, but all too often we forget. Opened or

Why a picture of Pointers? Well, to indicate the size of this very sturdy and safe outdoor pen. This pen can easily be fitted with a top, climbing trees and the like so that your cat can enjoy the outdoors. Additionally, an extension can be fitted leading from the pen to the window of your home so your cats can go in and out when they please. One thing, however. Obviously the chain link will keep dogs and cars away from your cats, but will not keep away fleas, flies and other pests. You, therefore, should be on the alert for these. Photo by the author with a "thank you" to Peter and Regina Bothner.

Only a very careless and uncaring cat owner would ever leave such things in such a way. That drain cleaner could kill a cat very swiftly as could the metal polish, ammonia and other substances. Please, tightly cap or seal such items after using them; if you own a cat you won't be sorry you took the time to care.

poorly closed containers for paint, turpentine, plant and/or lawn spray, automobile radiator antifreeze and the like invite trouble. While a cat may not eat one of these hazardous substances intentionally, if it gets something on its paws while walking it may develop secondary poisoning when it licks the paws clean. Improperly closed containers in the kitchen or bathroom cupboard for cleaners, polishes and the like invite similar misfortune inside the home proper.

Another danger indoors is the mothball. Cats love to bat things around, chase them, pick them up in their paws or mouth, wrestle with and dig at the object with their hind feet. Toys like mothballs that make noise when played with on fast, hard surfaces like bare wood or linoleum floors are favored. While the cat will probably not eat the mothball, the substance on it will get on the paws and when the cat cleans itself it will ingest this and get sick.

Some other things in the home which could be dangerous to your pet are sewing needles and pins that could be swallowed or become lodged in the paw, and plastic food wrap, cellophane and sponges which wreak havoc in the intestines if swallowed. There is always a danger with broken glass as it can easily become embedded in the pawpad. Garbage should be thrown out promptly, or at least kept in a cat-proof container, so that your cat can't get hold of bones, cellophane and other injurious things. Ingestion of aspirin and tobacco is extremely dangerous to cats and care should be taken that these substances not be left about. Most plants are toxic to cats if eaten; among these are the popular Christmas plants such as holly, mistletoe and poinsettia. Therefore, if you have cats, you should not have plants. Oftentimes people fail to realize that many commonly kept household plants are not merely hazardous but deadly to cats if eaten.

Although an indoor pet is much less susceptible to fleas than a free-roaming outdoor cat, the housecat still may come into contact with these pests. Fleas lay their eggs in your pet's bedding, in cracks in the floor or in any other dry place. The eggs may not hatch for a long time after they have been laid. For this reason your cat's sleeping quarters must be kept clean and the bedding should be frequently washed. Careful vacuuming in corners, cupboards and rugs will help to prevent any problems. Fleas are dangerous to your cat's health because, aside from the irritation of scratching, these tiny pests often transmit tapeworms.

Flies lay their eggs in moist areas, and because they often get into the house despite window screens, you should not allow your cat's wet food to remain in the dish for very long after feeding. This is especially important to remember in the summer, but it is a good rule to follow year-round as, if the fly eggs hatch, the resulting maggots can be most dangerous to your pet. Whenever possible, do not let your cat eat the flies it is bound to catch.

The housecat needs few requirements to enjoy its life indoors: regular changing of the litter and washing of the lit-

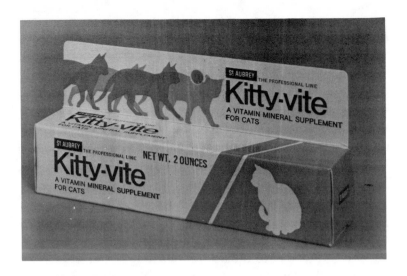

Another fine product that might be recommended to you or that you might want to try.

ter pan (with soap but not with possibly toxic disinfectant products), a scratchpost on which the cat can exercise and slough off its nails, some toys, fresh water, a small area to call its own and regular grooming to eliminate loose hair. If you have a dog remember that certain products safe for dogs are not safe for cats. Read all directions and instructions thoroughly before using any product. If in doubt, ask your veterinarian's advice.

Do not allow your pet access to damp areas as cats are as susceptible as we are to colds and respiratory ailments. The indoor cat can, barring catastrophic disease, live a full life with you if you take care to care for it properly. You have probably gotten a cat because you want the companionship and pleasures available to you from having it around. Show it affection regularly and it will return the same; your years together will be most pleasurable and rewarding.

TATTOOING

Tattooing cats as a means of identification is a relatively

35

recent development. The tattoos are usually put in the ear or groin and are done with tattooing needles and dye. As of this writing none of the cat registering bodies penalize tattooed cats in the show ring although one of these, the CFA, requires that the tattoo be no longer than 7 digits, no more than ½ " high and only put inside of the left flank. Thus, in the CFA alone, cats with ear tattoos are disqualified from show competition. Of course if your cat is to be a pet or breeder it does not matter where it is tattooed.

Not all veterinarians tattoo so you may have to make several inquiries before finding one who does. It is best done when the kitten is young. Your kitten will probably have to be brought to the doctor's office early in the morning and will most likely remain there all day. The risk of infection is negligible when tattooing is done properly by an experienced vet. You should expect to pay about $25 for this service.

Identification by tattoo is permanent, will last the life of your cat and makes it easy to positively identify your pet should it be lost or stolen. In many cases a breeder sells a kitten with a provision in the selling agreement that it be neutered by a certain time. It is an easy matter to verify that such a cat has in fact been altered by checking with the vet who performed the operation. Breeders also find tattoos useful to identify members of different litters.

As cats become more and more popular and increasingly more costly, it is quite probable that tattooing will be done more frequently.

DISCIPLINE AND TRAINING

Your cat was probably housebroken by its mother. Soon after the kit regularly ventured out of the nest it accompanied mom to the litter box, watched her do what was necessary and learned the box's purpose. It is extremely rare that by the time a kitten is with its new owner it has not learned how to use the litter pan, but if it hasn't you can place the kit in the pan whenever you catch it excreting. The cat's natural urge to dig and cover its wastes will motivate it to go in the pan.

A cat must trim its claws lest they become imbedded or infected. Cats trim their claws by scratching. The new kitten or cat may have been taught to use a scratching post instead of your furniture or rug to exercise its claws on. If not, this is easy for you to teach your pet. Whenever it exercises its claws, bring it over to the scratch place, put its front paws there and work them on the post. The urge to exercise should still be present and the cat will continue to scratch. A few repetitions of this and your cat will know to scratch there on its own. Basically a scratch place is wood covered over with carpeting. Normally it is upright, hence the term scratch post, but a carpeted board flat on the floor or slanted against a wall is equally good. Posts can be easily made at home or purchased at pet shops. Pet stores often also carry "cat castles," large cylinders completely covered over by carpeting with room inside for your pet to nap. Whichever you choose, it should be sturdy, with a base heavy enough to keep the post from being able to be tipped over, otherwise your pet will not use it but rather something which offers more resistance such as your sofa.

A most important vocal command is "No!" This should be said in a firm tone of voice to indicate your displeasure. Some people accompany this with a pointing finger. Your cat will soon learn to recognize this and associate it with incorrect behavior. Each time you discipline in this way you should look directly into your cat's face for maximum effect. You should always punish with your voice and not with your hand. Little can be accomplished by hitting your cat except frightening it and possibly getting yourself scratched. The "No!" command is usually sufficient to discipline whenever necessary. There is, however, one very useful disciplining tool that should be mentioned, and this is the water pistol. Cats do not like water squirted at them, and they will associate the squirt with a warning not to do whatever it is that caused them to be squirted. Water pistols have nice range, are quiet and do not physically harm your cat. They are very useful combined with the "No!".

While still a very young kitten a cat can be taught its name. This is probably the first word it should be taught. When you first begin to pet and handle your kitten, repeat its name over and over. After a while it will recognize it. Choose something simple that can be easily understood.

"Come" is another word command you should teach. Whenever your pet responds to this, reward it with a treat. This will enable your cat to associate coming with something pleasurable. The "Come" command is most useful should the cat get out of the house or car and need to be retrieved quickly.

Leash training is not difficult if the kitten is accustomed to it when young. A body harness is preferable to a neck collar since the restraining force is spread over a stronger area. Additionally, since a cat can easily get itself caught on something when wearing a collar, collaring a cat is not advised. Many people consider leash training of little value. They argue that since cats are box-trained they need not be walked like dogs, and it serves no purpose to walk them for the sake of exercise since they get all they need at home. They further point out that a cat's unnecessary exposure to outdoor parasites is risky and senseless.

Your cat can be taught tricks which will give both of you a lot of pleasure. They are independent, but cats do enjoy having fun with their owners if they choose the time. Retrieving is one trick that is easily taught. To start teaching your cat this trick, pick up your cat's favorite small plaything and toss it away from you (A crumpled ball of paper is ideal.) The cat will go over to it, investigate, probably bat it around and possibly pick it up in its mouth. Go over, pick up the plaything or paper ball and throw it a little away from you. Continue this a few times. Soon your cat will realize you are **playing with it and will bring the toy or** paper ball back to you; reward it as soon as it does. If you don't have any treats handy, pet and praise it lavishly.

There are many tricks you can teach your cat. If you want to pursue this further, get a copy of Margrit Lippman's *Cat Training* (TFH Publications #HS-1200) for step-by-step, illustrated training techniques for more than a dozen tricks. Remember when training to reward your cat for correct performance, to practice each trick regularly until it is mastered, not to train after meals or in excessively hot weather and, most important, to have fun!

GROOMING

When your cat was a kitten you should have accustomed it to the brush, stimulex or whatever else you chose to groom it with. Little kittens do not need much grooming care, but when they have been introduced to grooming while young will not struggle against it when mature. Brushing should be done regularly and should be a pleasurable experience for both of you. Regular coat care keeps the fur free of ticks and fleas, prevents the coat from matting and helps to remove the dandruff flakes that develop when the cat renews the skin beneath the fur. Twice yearly, when preparing for the summer and winter, your cat will thin or fill out its coat. This is less noticeable in cats that are kept indoors than in those that live outside, but it nevertheless occurs. Brushing will remove the excess fur and at these times should be done daily; this will also help to prevent hairballs which form in the cat's stomach when it swallows hair following self-grooming.

The front claws should be clipped as needed. There are several types of nailclippers available; be sure to get one suited for cats and not for large dogs. The thin red line in the nail, the quick, is where the vein begins. Do not cut into this as it is very painful to your pet and it will bleed from

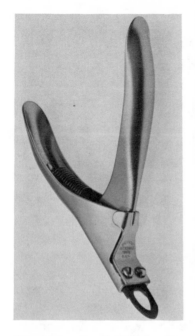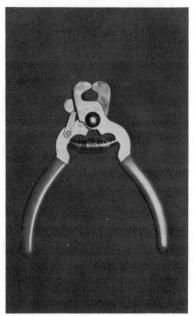

Two types of nail clippers. There is no reason to choose one over the other except that you should use the one you are most comfortable with.

a cut here. If you have not yet learned how to trim properly or if you are afraid of hurting your cat, just trim off the very tip where the nail is most pointed. When you bring your cat to the vet for its first shots and checkup, ask him to show you how to properly care for the nails. The claws on the hind paws rarely need to be clipped except that they must be trimmed prior to show competition.

The ears should be wiped out with cotton and mineral oil occasionally. The accumulation of brown matter in the ears indicates the presence of mites which need to be eradicated. Your vet will treat this the first time and will show you how to provide follow-up care. Never put anything way down into the ear canal. Cats' ears are very sensitive, and you can permanently injure your pet if you carelessly probe in its ears.

Cats' eyes rarely need care unless diseased. The matter

40

that daily appears in the corners is usually cleaned by the cat after it has dried. It is not unlike the "sand" we humans find in our eyes upon rising. If your cat is lazy about eye care, you can wipe any matter away with a tissue.

Sometimes you cannot give your cat a water bath. Dry shampoo cleans without water and really does clean out the coat. Pet shops offer a good variety of dry shampoos.

The best rule about bathing is that if the cat needs a bath, bathe it. Human shampoo is too harsh for a cat but many cat shampoos are currently available. Wash your cat in warm water. Completely rinse out the soap so that the skin oils are not dried out later, and thoroughly towel-dry your pet to protect it from catching cold.

ADMINISTERING MEDICATION

Cats will not usually eat or drink food to which medication has been added so it is necessary that you know how to efficiently give a pill or liquid to your cat. The easiest way to give liquid medicine is with a plastic dropper (using a glass dropper is not suggested as it might shatter if bitten). Put the dropper in the corner of the mouth and squeeze the bulb gently so that you give a small amount the cat can

Just a few of the many different cat shampoos available. Always use a shampoo specifically formulated for use on cats.

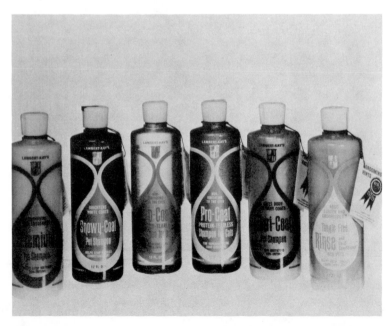

swallow without choking. Repeat this until the total amount has been accepted. You may even be able to pour the medicine in from a teaspoon, but many cats won't cooperate for this.

There are several ways to give a pill; I've found the following method to be the easiest. Secure your cat next to your body and grasp its head from above. With four fingers on one side of its mouth and your thumb on the other, open the mouth and tilt the head back and up. With your free hand pop in the pill as far back into the mouth as you can. Close your pet's mouth—this will cause it to swallow. A few pats, kind words and a treat will help your cat to regain its dignity. You may find it easier to give a pill coated with butter or fish oil or supplement; this is especially useful when giving a large capsule. Keep in mind that the more gentle yet efficient you are the more tolerable the situation will be for both of you.

TAKING YOUR CAT'S TEMPERATURE

Lubricate the tip of a rectal thermometer with vaseline. Take your cat's tail near the base and gently lift it up to expose the anus. With your free hand gently insert the thermometer about one and a half to two inches. Hold your cat and leave the thermometer in about three minutes to get an accurate reading. These may seem like the longest three minutes you have ever spent with your cat, especially if it's your first time at this. Remain calm and comfort kitty the whole time because she's not enjoying this any more than you are. Be careful not to touch the tip upon withdrawal as this may affect the reading. A cat's normal temperature is about 101°F; should this vary, illness is indicated. As with giving a pill, help your cat to regain its dignity when you are finished.

CARE OF THE OLDER CAT

Cats, like us, become aged. They slow down, don't play

as much as they once did, sleep more, perhaps become more finicky in their eating habits and may have occasional bladder "accidents." Just as among humans, cats' lifespans vary, and some cats age more quickly than others and some die earlier than others. It is very difficult to establish precisely what is a normal lifespan for a cat, but it may be said to range from eight to fifteen years. Chances of longevity increase with proper care and nutrition, and we often hear of cats living into their late teens or twenties—especially if they have spent their lives indoors and were not left to run free.

Successful research in nutrition and in treatment of diseases has greatly helped to increase the lifespans of today's pets. Neglect, serious illness, poor food and poor housing are some of the things which shorten our cats' lives. There is no reason, barring catastrophic illness or accident, why our cats cannot live long and happy lives.

As our cats age they may have problems with rheumatism, arthritis, heart disease, prostatitis or kidney infection, but modern medicine has made it possible to mollify the debilitating effects of these. Deaf, blind or partially-blind cats may require a bit more care when they get older, but proper care and kind consideration of any older cat's needs—especially for rest and not as much strenuous play with us as when it was young—should enable the older cat to live out its life with us comfortably.

Ailments and Afflictions

SYMPTOMS OF ILLNESS

A cat normally has a good appetite, clear eyes, good muscle tone, an alert expression, firm stools and a glossy coat. Should any of these change, something is probably bothering your cat. Do not be alarmed if your pet refuses a meal or two as this is common, but more consecutive food refusal than this is often a sign of illness. Diarrhea is another common indication that all is not well. At the least this indicates the possibility of worms. An out of condition coat may suggest dietary deficiency or the presence of external parasites.

Learn what is a normal, healthy condition for your cat and regularly examine it. Early detection of a problem may make required treatment easier and will certainly check any disease before it becomes serious.

VIRAL DISEASES

Viral diseases are the great cat killers. One, properly named infectious feline panleucopenia but also known as FIE, cat fever, feline distemper and feline enteritis, attacks the cat's intestines. Its onset is characterized by general listlessness, food refusal, high temperature, weakness, vomiting and sometimes diarrhea. The afflicted cat may hang its head over a water dish without drinking. Because this disease attacks so swiftly it is easy to mistake for poisoning. If ever you notice these symptoms in your cat contact your veterinarian for immediate diagnosis and treatment.

Panleucopenia is passed by contact with contaminated areas, infected animals or their feces, or through an intermediary such as a human, dog, fly or flea that has come into contact with the disease. While cat fever is transmittable by human or canine, it is not infectious to them. Because the germs can endure for a long time it is not considered safe to bring an unvaccinated cat into any home where distemper has been until about six months have elapsed and old bedding, feeding dishes, litter pans and the like have been disposed of.

For some time there has been a vaccine available to protect cats against this killer, and this is usually administered when a cat is around eight weeks old. Booster shots may be given on a yearly basis. Because kittens are especially vulnerable to FIE, immunization at the proper age is a must.

Two additional highly contagious viral diseases are pneumonitis and viro-rhinotracheitis. Their symptoms resemble those of a severe cold or flu in humans: watery eyes, shivering, sneezing, runny nose, sore throat and overall achiness. Pneumonitis is spread through the air and by contact with things that have been sneezed on.

Because an affected cat's nose is stopped up it cannot smell its food and will often not want to eat. This is not good; the weakening effect this has on the cat is dangerous and it may become necessary to force-feed the cat to keep its resistance and strength up.

Early detection and treatment is important because while pneumonitis is deadly it does not act as quickly as panleucopenia and can be checked by antibiotics. After treatment by a doctor, the afflicted cat should be isolated, well cared for, warm and free from drafts.

A vaccine is available that does not, however, offer permanent protection against these diseases and which, therefore, needs to be given periodically. Your vet will advise you in this regard.

Cats are also subject to colds which are transmittable from one cat to another. Symptoms, although less severe, are often the same as those for the previously mentioned serious diseases, so proper diagnosis and prescription by a veterinarian are advised.

Rabies is another viral disease that afflicts cats. It has no known cure but is controllable. Bats, skunks and foxes are known carriers; country or farm cats which have the opportunity to encounter these are therefore most susceptible. An open wound or cut that comes into contact with the saliva of a rabies-infected animal is all it takes for a cat (or any other mammal) to contract the disease.

Cats can be vaccinated against rabies and certain state and county agencies often offer this protection free of charge. Proof of protection against this disease is often required for feline travel or shipping.

In recent years feline viral leukemia has emerged as yet another deadly enemy. Medical research is working on a vaccine against this menace but as yet with inconclusive results. Oftentimes, you will see a breeder advertising his stock as FeLV neg. This means his cats have been tested for this disease and found to be free from it. Since leukemia is almost always fatal, a preventive will hopefully be found soon.

URINARY PROBLEMS

Frequent unsuccessful attempts to urinate, straining to urinate or the presence of blood in passed urine indicates that a cat's urinary tract may be blocked. Should you notice any of these symptoms, or if your cat acts extremely uneasy or cries out when picked up, there is a good possibility that it is suffering from bladder disorder. If this condition is not promptly attended to by a veterinarian the affected cat will quickly die from uremic poisoning as the body tissues absorb bladder overflow. Even if bladder disorder is not found to be the problem, it is far better to have made a diagnostic visit to the doctor than to have waited until it was too late. Routine check of the litter pan will indicate absence or presence of urine there and will aid you in catching any problems before they become serious.

OBESITY

A fat cat has more strain than normal placed on its joints and heart, is more susceptible to viral or bacterial infections and is a poor anesthetic risk. A housecat can only become overweight through human negligence since it does not get the opportunity to raid garbage cans and fatten up on scraps outdoors. Therefore, don't overindulge your pet with treats but keep it healthy and in top condition.

The cure for obesity is to feed less and make the cat partially nourish itself off of its stored fat. Reduced caloric intake will have no ill effect on your cat provided a good quality balanced diet is fed.

SKIN AILMENTS

As soon as you notice any irregularity in your cat's coat you should have the animal checked. Early detection, diagnosis and treatment are important in the arrest, control and cure of skin diseases, especially since some of them are highly contagious.

Ringworm is a fungus disease that can appear on any part of the body. It first appears as an oval or round spot from which the hair has fallen out, and as it spreads the size of the naked area becomes larger. Recent advances in medicine have produced new drugs extremely effective against this annoying ailment. A particularly unpleasant feature of this disease is its ability to be freely transmitted between feline and human. Thorough vacuuming and scrubbing of the home are thus very important in controlling its spread. Bedding, both yours and the cat's, should be washed frequently. An infected cat should be isolated until cured. Your vet will prescribe proper medication and dosage, and if you follow his directions faithfully the ringworm will be eliminated.

There are other fungus diseases which may afflict your pet with oozing sores. Prompt diagnosis and treatment will cure these.

Allergic reaction to particular foods, medications (such as flea powders, sprays or collars) or fibers (some cats do not live well with nylon or other synthetic carpeting) are a common cause of skin ailments as are tick and/or flea bites, bee stings and vitamin deficiency or overdosage. Unfortunately, determining the cause of a particular allergy is often difficult, and a vet may have to make many tests before arriving at the correct answer and prescribing the proper treatment.

FLEAS AND TICKS

Regular inspection of your pets will keep potential problems under control. Both ticks and fleas can be seen with the naked eye. Black specks in a cat's chin whiskers indicate the presence of fleas as they use this area for their toilet. The fleas themselves are usually found around the anus, eyes and mouth since they feed in these areas.

Fleas are dark brown or black. They are especially troublesome during the warmer months and cause irritating itching, may spread fungus and/or ringworm and often serve as intermediate hosts for tapeworms. Cat fleas are not the same as dog fleas, and a cat owner is not likely to encounter dog fleas unless he owns a dog as well.

You should vacuum frequently if you live in an area where fleas are common. This is most necessary because young fleas develop in dust in dry areas such as under the sofa, between cracks in floorboards, under rugs and in other similar places. Fleas' eggs can lie dormant for months until proper conditions are present for hatching. For this reason flea powder should be sprinkled under carpets and furniture and left there. Your pet's bedding should be regularly washed and treated with flea powder as well. Brushing your cat daily will also help to prevent the pests from establishing themselves.

Fleas can be controlled by daily application of flea powder and brushing out of the cat's coat. A bath with flea shampoo followed by a thorough grooming session may be sufficient to eliminate the parasites. Your cat should not be bathed too often, however, as this dries out the natural oils protecting the coat.

Reinfestation is possible, especially through contact with other pets that are allowed to go outside and come back indoors or through fleas you bring into the house on your clothing.

Ticks are dangerous because they can cause blood poisoning, fever or paralysis. They burrow their heads into the cat's flesh and gorge on its blood. Usually they are found on the head and neck where the cat cannot reach them. To remove a tick, grasp it with your fingers or a tweezers as close to the cat's body as possible. Try to get the head and mouth and not just the tick's body. Pull straight back gently and not too abruptly. It is very important that the head be removed lest infection develop. Tick and flea powder applied directly to the tick will cause it to die and fall off in a few hours. You must be careful when using commercial tick and flea powder that it is safe for cats. Do not use matches, lighted cigarettes, kerosene or gasoline to remove the tick; while these will surely kill the pest they will also burn the cat. After the tick has been removed, clean the area with antiseptic solution from your veterinarian. Watch the area for a week or so to make sure it is healing properly and no abscess is developing.

Ticks are a rural problem. They can be dealt with easily, however, and early treatment will prevent infestation.

WORMS

Whenever you suspect or have already confirmed the fact that your cat has worms you should bring a stool sample to your vet for examination. He will probably suggest that the cat be brought in after he has analyzed the stool. Medication will be prescribed for the type of worm present, and the dosage will be based on the age and size of your cat.

Worming preparations are strong stuff; they must be to kill the worms. For this reason you should never worm your cat yourself. Incorrect dosage could make your pet seriously ill or even kill it if given over a long period.

Worm infestation is debilitating, detracts from a cat's overall appearance and condition and, if serious, makes a cat more susceptible to serious disease. A fecal analysis by a veterinarian will determine the presence of worms.

Roundworms live in the intestines and feed on partially digested food. Some of the eggs laid are passed out in the stool. Cats that use the same litter box can infect each other when an uninfected cat licks its paws clean and thus ingests the teensy eggs which later hatch inside it.

Usually we find a curled up roundworm in vomit or stool. They are pointed at both ends and yellowish white in color.

Tapeworms are not as easily diagnosed as roundworms in a fecal analysis. A sure sign that a cat is infected with them is the presence of white rice-grain like particles around the home in those areas the cat frequents. The tapeworm is a segmented animal. Its head remains attached to the intestine wall, but as eggs are produced the worm sheds the egg-producing segments of its body which are passed out of the host's anus. The rice-grain like pieces you find are these egg sacs. If an uninfested cat eats these it can then become infected. Again, this most usually occurs when cats share the same litter pan. Regular vacuuming of the home is advised if you have a cat afflicted with tapeworm. The implanted head of the tapeworm is very tenacious and may take some time to dislodge and kill. The strong medicine needed to rid your pet of the pest may make it feel out of sorts for a while, but your vet will prescribe proper and safe dosage for your individual cat.

EAR PROBLEMS

Ear canker is a condition frequently found in cats. It is

caused by mites which breed in the dust, dirt and wax of a cat's ears. Regular cleaning of the ears with cotton swabs dipped in mineral oil is the best prevention. Once ear mites have developed they can quickly spread to all the cats in a household, and serious mite infestation can harm a cat's hearing and affect its balance.

Mite infestation is characterized by dark brown crumbly matter visible in the ear canal. Even when this crusty material is not visible mites can still be present since the deeper reaches of the ear canal are not visible to the naked eye. If your cat constantly scratches its ears or shakes its head the presence of ear mites is indicated. Bad cases require twice daily treatment (with some preparations at least) which may not be pleasant for the owner, but the cat afflicted with mites is even more uncomfortable. Since prevention is so easy, our cats should not suffer because of our laziness.

Care must be taken when using a swab that it is not inserted too deeply into the ear canal. When mites are suspected or when the cat is taken to the vet for a regular checkup, the doctor will check and clean the ears as part of the examination and treatment. He will be glad to demonstrate to you the proper way to clean your cat's ears and treat them for mites if present.

HAIRBALLS

All cats ingest the loose hair that comes off their bodies when they groom themselves. These hairs accumulate in the intestine where they form into wads or balls (hence the term "hairballs") and are passed out with stool or vomited. Regular brushing of your pet, especially when it twice yearly sheds and renews its coat, will help to alleviate this annoying problem. A diet supplemented with fish oil or choline and inositol will enable your cat to more easily pass hairballs.

First Aid

First aid is assistance given before professional help can be gotten. It needs to be administered calmly, quickly and efficiently. You ought to have a feline first aid kit in your home which can also be brought along when your cat travels with you. The kit should contain antiseptic first aid cream, sterile non-stick pads, sterile cotton, hydrogen peroxide, bandaging tape, tweezers, scissors and mineral oil. A blanket and flashlight are also useful. You will notice that all of the above items belong in your car and home anyway. Should you, a member of your family or a guest or passenger ever require medical assistance you will be prepared. Remember that the better taken care of an injured party is before getting a doctor's help, the better the injured's chances are of a successful recovery.

ARTIFICIAL RESPIRATION

Should you need to resuscitate a cat you must act quickly since a delay of even a few minutes in getting the animal to breathe will cause irreversible brain damage. There are two forms of artificial respiration which may be used: mouth to mouth resuscitation and the pressure method. Both methods require the same initial preparations. First clear the mouth and throat of mucus, food or any other matter. Then grip and pull out the tongue; this will be easier if you hold it with a piece of cloth such as your handkerchief or shirt.

Mouth to mouth is simple, quick and efficient. Take a breath of air, cover the cat's mouth and nose with your mouth and hand and exhale into its mouth. Remember that you are not blowing up a balloon and that a cat's lung capacity is not so great as our own. You may have to repeat this a few times and you may, after exhaling into the cat, have to push down firmly behind its elbow to get it breathing. I know from personal experience that this method works and that it is easy to perform.

The second method works through the application of pressure. Push down firmly behind the elbow for three seconds; this compresses the lungs. Release for three seconds and continue until the cat begins to breathe on its own. After this has occurred assist it further by applying pressure in time with the cat's own breathing rate until it appears comfortable.

Keep the animal warm with a blanket or, if one is not available, with your coat, jacket or shirt after the cat is breathing normally. Contact a veterinarian for further instructions.

BLEEDING

Bleeding may come from an artery, vein or capillary. Loss of blood must be stopped as quickly as possible. If you see blood spurting from a wound at regular intervals (with each heartbeat), an artery has been cut. This is the most severe and most serious type of bleeding and you will have to apply a tourniquet to stop it. Use a piece of cloth such as a handkerchief. Don't waste time looking for something; rip your shirt if you have to, but act swiftly. The material should be tied loosely and tightened with a stick. If no stick is available use a pencil, pen or even merely a twisting of the cloth held in place with your hand. Apply the tourniquet as close as possible to the wound on the side closest the heart. It should be applied tight enough to control the bleeding but no tighter. Leave the tourniquet on eight or so minutes and then loosen it for three or four minutes. Whenever you need a tourniquet you need a veterinarian. If you are alone with the cat you will have to call the doctor yourself; it is better if someone can do this for you so you can stay with the animal the whole time until you reach the doctor's.

Any arterial bleeding you might encounter will probably appear in the limbs. This is fortunate as you cannot apply a tourniquet to the neck or body proper. If there is an arterial wound in either of these areas you will have to use the compression method described below to control the bleeding and will then have to contact a doctor for further help.

Dripping or oozing bleeding is from a vein or capillary and is easier to control than arterial bleeding. Apply firm pressure over the area with a clean cloth. Rip your shirt if you have to, but don't waste time looking for bandaging material. Hold the compress for several minutes over the wound and release; you should notice a greatly reduced blood flow. One or two applications of pressure should be sufficient; if bleeding has not decreased, you will have to wrap the area and contact a vet for assistance.

SHOCK

Shock results from reduced blood supply to the brain. Symptoms include slow heartbeat, reduced body temperature and hyperventilation. Clear the mouth and throat of any obstructions so that the windpipe is clear. The most common blockage is the tongue. Next stop any bleeding. Keep the cat warm and elevate the hind area slightly to keep the head lower than the heart. Now get to a veterinarian quickly for follow-up care.

If the shock is electric shock, do not touch the animal until you have disconnected the power source of the shocking instrument lest you injure yourself. Give artificial respiration if necessary, treat as above and contact the vet.

CARING FOR WOUNDS

Any bleeding must be stopped before proceeding further. To further prevent infection, clean the area with warm soapy water, hydrogen peroxide or antibacterial solution and dry it as thoroughly as possible. Bandage with a non-sticking sterile pad next to the skin and add gauze pads to this padding. Tape the bandage in place taking care not to make it too tight. To prevent it from slipping, some hair-covered area on all sides must be taped. Again, if proper materials aren't available use what you have on hand until later when you can redo whatever has to be done.

If the cut is severe, either very long or very deep, temporarily align the wound edges with butterfly closures or tape before bandaging. These wounds will require veterinary care.

Cuts in the pawpads should be cleaned well and checked for foreign matter embedded there before bandaging. Broken glass is a common cause of pad injury. If there is much swelling in the injured area after a while, it is possible a pus socket has formed that will need to be lanced and cleaned.

Puncture wounds, such as animal bites, must be watched especially closely. Abscesses can form in these deeper wounds and pus can collect. Inflammation around the wound indicates infection and your vet should examine the wound if this has occurred.

Gunshot wounds will cause bleeding and shock. Treat the injured cat for these and bring it to the doctor for further care.

Abscesses can be treated by removing part or all of a scab and encouraging the wound to ooze. Clean the area well and keep the wound open. Don't let a scab re-form until the infection has been eliminated.

FRACTURES

A veterinarian will ultimately have to handle a broken bone; what you need to do is safely protect the injured area and get the cat to the doctor quickly. If the broken bone sticks through the skin (a compound or open fracture) don't move it as you could tear blood vessels, muscle or nerve tissue. If you suspect a break but can't see it (a closed or simple fracture), you can splint the break. Use a sturdy material for the splints; board is best but a thick newspaper roll will do. Put one splint on each side of the break and wrap it with tape or cloth. Do not bandage too tightly yet firmly enough that the splint does not easily come off. As soon as possible have the break x-rayed by your vet so that he can determine how to best repair the fracture.

MOVING AN INJURED CAT

This is best accomplished on a stretcher which can be a wooden board, sturdy piece of cardboard or a shirt buttoned with two mop handles through the sleeves and body. Before moving an injured animal check for bleeding, breathing difficulties, shock and fractures. Always treat these conditions before doing anything else.

HEAT PROSTRATION

The most common cause of heat injury to a cat is being locked in a car without ventilation. The inside temperature quickly rises, maybe as much as forty degrees higher than the temperature outside. A less common cause of feline heat prostration occurs when the animal is unknowingly closed off in a closet or attic. The signs of this affliction include panting, foaming at the mouth or collapse. Cool down the cat's body temperature gradually with water. Take the cat's temperature regularly, every five minutes or so. If the injured animal is comatose, reduce the temperature as above and then bring the cat to a veterinarian.

BURNS

It is fortunate that cats most often are burned on their feet since burns here are easiest to treat, whether caused by fire or chemicals. A common cause of burned paws is contact with the still-hot heating element of an electric range. The injured foot may be held in very cool water for about twenty minutes. First-aid cream should be applied liberally

57

to the injured area after this and then a non-sticking pad is applied over the medicated area taking care that no part of the injured area is not covered. Further bandage the area with pads and tape. Because burned tissue swells, do not apply the bandage too tightly. The bandage will have to be changed regularly and medication reapplied.

If the burn is in an area other than the paw, it should be washed with cool water for about twenty minutes and then treated with medication as above. Bandaging may be a problem and you should seek veterinary assistance.

In cases where burns are severe or cover a large area, professional help should be gotten as quickly as possible after first aid has been given.

POISONING

The most common cause of feline poisoning are plants and chemicals. Because so many commonly kept houseplants are toxic to cats it is better that if you have one you don't have the other. Some of the more common chemical poisons are found in insecticides, fungicides, herbicides, rat, snail and slug poisons and cleaning compounds. You can help to prevent accidental poisoning of your pet (and your children too) by keeping these substances tightly closed in an inaccessible, secure place. Prevention is the best defense against a needless poisoning.

The usual symptoms of poisoning include vomiting, incoordinate movement and convulsions. It is very difficult to treat poisoning without knowing what caused it. You will have to call your cat's doctor for help. If you know what the substance was that affected your cat, by all means indicate this to the vet as he may be able to suggest first aid you can perform before bringing the cat to him.

OTHER PROBLEMS

A fish hook near the eye should be removed by a veterinarian; in other locations you can probably remove it yourself (except of course if it is lodged in the throat). Push the hook through the skin until the barb is exposed. Cut the shank with a pliers, or a scissors will do if you cut near to the handle where you have the most power, and the barb will fall off. Pull the shank out of the skin the same way it entered the skin. Treat this as any other puncture wound.

If you notice thread hanging from your cat's mouth don't pull it out. There is a good chance a needle has been swallowed and has become lodged in your pet's throat or even in its stomach. Look in the cat's mouth; if you can see the other end of the thread there is obviously no problem, but if you can't see the other end suspect the worst. Call your vet who will probably require that the cat be fluoroscoped so he can see exactly where the needle is before removing it. You can easily prevent this kind of problem by making sure your sewing tools are always put away securely.

Frostbite usually occurs on the feet, tail or ears. Apply moist heat to the afflicted area with a towel or cloth and repeat frequently. Dry the injured area and protect it with non-stick bandages.

An encounter with a skunk is usually no fun for a feline. Wash the cat with tomatoes or tomato juice and then bathe it thoroughly with soap and water. Much of the odor will be eliminated after this although a residual amount may remain for a while.

A meeting with a porcupine is a sticky situation. Each quill must be removed, and this is very painful. For this reason your vet should do it, and he may well have to anesthetize the cat first.

A cat that has taken a serious fall should first be given artificial respiration if necessary and then treated for bleeding and fractures. A vet should be contacted immediately after first aid has been administered.

Sometimes it is necessary to restrict or confine a cat. A cage such as the one pictured provides ample room for the cat to exercise and rest in and the screen door enables the confined cat to see out and not feel apart from the rest of the family. A cage like this is also often used for matings. Photo by the author.

Breeding

BREEDING ETHICS

Responsible breeders produce healthy well-adjusted cats. Kitten-mill breeders, those breeding to make a quick sale to an unknowing buyer, often produce very inferior specimens. The kittens are often so sickly that they have to be put down, and the queens are so overbred and debilitated that they die prematurely at a young age.

Breeding "just to see what comes out" shows little sensitivity or regard for life. One has only to visit the local ASPCA or Humane Society to see a large number of beautiful kittens up for adoption because their owners satisfied their curiosity irresponsibly.

Conscientious breeders do not allow their animals to be bred to cats of unknown quality as regards health, temperament and type. The profit to be made from a breeding fee may interest and entice the careless breeder, but many take very seriously the phrase "To approved studs/queens only."

The costs involved in breeding even inferior cats sold cheaply leaves only a small profit from the sale of the kittens. This shouldn't even be considered as a means of making money, but, unfortunately, some people only realize this after their unrewarding personal experiences. Because money is the primary goal of mass-production breeders, they usually miss the joy and excitement that comes with responsible breeding.

The goal of every breeder should be to produce cats of the highest quality in temperament, hardiness and conformation. Ethical breeders do not allow carriers of a serious fault to be bred. When breeding to cats of another cattery each breeder has to trust that the other's cats are perfectly healthy.

Since mating arrangements are usually made well in advance of the mating, the owner of the stud has to honor this commitment at the appropriate time. It is unfair to the owner of the female to have to seek out another male at the last minute or to have to postpone breeding his in-condition and in-season female because the stud's owner withdraws from the agreement at the last minute. Of course if either the tom or the queen goes out of condition right before the intended mating, the responsible owner will notify the other breeder of this and reschedule the breeding.

DECIDING TO BREED YOUR CAT(S)

Before involving yourself with the breeding of cats you must carefully ascertain in advance whether or not you will have the time to devote to it. The cattery must be kept clean at all times. Feeding your pets takes time as well, especially when you are preparing special diets. You must also have the space. An extra bedroom, an enclosed porch or a sitting room are easily converted into a cattery. Breeding well also requires money. Superior quality foods must be given regularly to keep your stock in top condition. Regular trips to the vet with a large number of cats are not inexpensive even if your vet allows for "group rates." When you are starting your breeding program you should purchase the best quality stock you can afford. This expense is not so great when you consider that it is spread out over the lifespan of the cat, but the initial cost is nonetheless substantial when paid out in one lump sum. These are some of the tangible elements to consider when determining whether or not to breed.

Another much more subtle question must be answered before proceeding with a breeding program: do you know enough about quality and desired type to produce the same? As a novice breeder you will learn to develop your powers of comparison and observation. Experience can teach much. Go to cat shows. Compare the cats you see to the ideal in your head. If you already own a cat you wish to breed, look for a mate that is strongest in areas where yours is weakest. After studying your breed for a while, you will prefer certain animals to others. When good reasons for your preferences can be found, reasons that will be supported by experienced breeders and fanciers, you are on your way to becoming a good breeder yourself.

WHEN TO BREED

A cat may reach its sexual maturity before it is a year old. As a general rule, a female should not be bred earlier than this. If she has frequently come into season before her first birthday, and if you have intended to breed her rather than have her spayed, you should consult your vet. He may suggest that she be bred at this early age because of the possibility that she might develop cysts on her ovaries if not mated.

The too young queen may have difficulty with her first litter. She may devote insufficient time to her kits due to her inexperience, and she may not be mature enough to be a good mother. Because she is still growing herself, the nutrients in her food will be used to sustain her needs rather than to produce rich and sufficient quantity milk for the kittens.

A female older than one year makes a very good mother. She is strong and vibrant and will be able to rear healthy young. She can deliver easier than an older queen because the bone and cartilage in her pelvic area is still elastic and able to stretch during labor. Provided that she is well nourished, she will be able to properly provide for her young.

Most breeders recommend that the female in season be mated around the third day of her estrus as this seems to be the ideal time of conception. Additionally, she tends to be less excitable at this time than she is on the first and second days.

A male is usually able to service a female by the time he is nine months old; some males are ready earlier and others even later. The cat associations will not register kittens sired by a very young male so be sure to check the regulations of those organizations you intend to enter your litter in. A younger male that shows interest in breeding may be tried, but make sure that the intended female is not difficult. An unpleasant experience at his first mating attempt may discourage the younger male from further breedings. After the male is a year old he can normally be easily and confidently bred. While a mature male is always able to mate and does not go into season as a female does, he should only be bred when in top condition.

METHODS OF BREEDING

Inbreeding reduces breeding to its simplest form and certain results can be fairly accurately predicted and produced. This method concentrates and intensifies weaknesses already present in the line but does not add additional faults to the resultant offspring. The converse is also true, however, and many breeders inbreed to strengthen virtues in their line before outcrossing. Once a fault or virtue becomes established in the line it is very difficult to get rid of. Thus, this method of breeding must be used very carefully to obtain the best results. Inbreeding involves father-daughter, mother-son and brother-sister matings. Brothers and sisters are the most genetically alike members of a family and are often mated when both are particularly fine.

It is obviously necessary to inbreed when establishing a new breed as this is the only way to establish type because so few representatives of the new breed exist in the beginning.

Backcrossing is a form of inbreeding in which the best daughter (or son) of a first litter is bred back to her (or his) sire (or mother). The best daughter (or son) of this mating is then mated back to her (or his) father (or mother). This continues until the desired results are achieved.

An accident to either the tom or the queen could destroy the line if new. For this reason inbreeding is often used as a precautionary step when a line is not yet established.

Linebreeding is the mating of not closely related members of the same family such as grandfather to granddaughter or uncle to niece. It is not considered as extreme a form of breeding as inbreeding.

Outcrossing is the mating of cats that have no common ancestors within five generations. This breeding method is used when a breeder attempts to fix desirable qualities of another line in his own future stock. When a breeder gets a good level of quality from a particular outcross he often repeats this mating again. Both lines are thereby strengthened (if both breeders use the offspring in their breeding programs) and the breed as a whole is enhanced. Outcrossing only adds qualities, whether they be good ones or bad, but does not change what is already there.

Compensation breeding is a term used to describe mating one animal lacking in a particular respect to another specimen strong in the same area. The offspring produced should include some young which show the desired improvement.

KEEPING YOUR OWN BREEDING STOCK

As a breeder you may not choose to keep your own stud. There are advantages and disadvantages in whichever decision you reach. You will know more about your own male, his faults and strengths, than you will about another breeder's. Likewise, you will know more about his offspring than that of another male's. It is easier to breed your own female when you keep the male; you can even choose the exact time to mate them. Test matings can easily be made which will increase your knowledge of your tom's type. When you do not wish to breed your female, however, you will have to keep her separated from your male which can be difficult when both are housecats. If you keep more than one whole male in the house, there is a good chance that they will fight regularly. Finally, you do not have as wide a selection of studs available to breed to your female as you would if you selected from among other breeders' males.

There are more inferior females used for breeding than inferior males. This is true because while many females are mated few males are. It is difficult to keep a whole male in the house. His mating urge is constant and very strong. He will forever try to get out of the house and will continually attempt to mate any females inside the home as well. The natural instinct of the male to mark territory with his strong-smelling urine makes it impossible to allow him run of the house unless the highly offensive odor of his spray is inoffensive to you.

Many stud males lead miserable lives cooped up in small areas. They rarely have the opportunity to play and socialize with their owners or other cats. If you intend to keep a whole male, allow him sufficient territory to call his own and keep him happy, vibrant and well-adjusted with regular attention. In this way he will produce quality offspring. When you no longer breed him and have him neutered he can live out his life as a loving and lovable housepet.

A whole female is easier to keep than a whole male. She may spray, but even if she does her odor is not so pungent. She will of course call when in season. Some breeds are very loud callers while others are quite quiet when calling. While a female will come into season several times a year, this does not last long and she soon is her normal self.

The vigorous stud male requires a high-quality diet in sufficient quantity with good multi-mineral and multi-vitamin supplements added. This ensures that he will keep his condition and sperm count high. He should also have ample room to exercise freely. Human attention will keep his temperament good. A stud should not be allowed to become overweight as this will affect his prowess. After he has been bred several times he should be rested for a while before being rebred; this gives him time to fully restore himself. The coat quality of a tom is a good indication of his general condition, so this should be regularly watched. The quality of his recent offspring also serves as a guide to his powers.

A fertile female produces a large number of eggs and is able to produce rich milk. Breeder queens require a good diet. Calcium supplements are important as they help to ensure that the queen will produce enough rich milk to feed her young. The female should not be fat when bred as this condition makes it harder for her to give birth. She may spot a bit around the house when in season or already bred, but there is no reason for her not to have run of the house up to the time of delivery. A few days before the expected delivery date you may want to confine her to a breeding pen or room.

It is generally agreed that cats of both sexes should be bred regularly to maintain full fertility. For females this means once (some catpeople argue twice) a year. Males can be mated several times per month but must be rested regularly.

BREEDING ARRANGEMENTS BETWEEN CATTERIES

If you elect to use another breeder's stud you have a wide selection from which to choose. When you decide on a proper tom for your queen you have to choose carefully. It is cheaper in the long run to ship your female and pay a stud fee to another breeder whenever your queen is mated than it is to keep and maintain your own stud. You will probably see some of the offspring produced by another's male and can evaluate him in this way, but what you will be shown are the better kittens and not the poorer offspring. Thus, a true judging of the male's success as a stud is not often possible. There may have been only a few superior or even above average kittens produced by him; the majority, those you will not get the opportunity to see, may have been quite average or even inferior. Of course, if you are looking to breed pet quality kittens only this is not important, but if you are breeding regularly you should be doing so only to improve the breed stock and not to mass-produce kittens. Unless the intended stud is nearby, you will have to ship your female to him. This is sometimes difficult to arrange if one or both of the breeders is unable to travel to the airport or if the female cat travels poorly. Although slight, there is a chance that the female shipped to the tom will not conceive due to the stress of travel or the strange surroundings.

There is a tendency, especially among novice breeders, to select a stud on the basis of his show wins. This is not always the best practice to follow since less-frequently shown males are often superior breeders who consistently produce choice offspring.

If you have elected to breed your cat to another breeder's you will exchange pedigrees. Current photos may also be exchanged at this time. After all preliminary arrangements have been satisfactorily agreed to by both parties the contract is signed.

A written agreement is the only certain guarantee against future misunderstandings. It should cover all the various aspects of the intended breeding. The stud fee must be clearly stated. The price often depends on the stud's show wins and/or the quality of the offspring he has previously produced.

The usual stud fee is a straight money arrangement. Sometimes a kitten is accepted as full payment of the fee but this is extremely rare. Often a kitten is considered partial settlement in combination with a reduced cash amount. It is most uncommon for a stud owner to pay to mate his male with another breeder's female. In these cases the tom's owner is invariably looking for one of the offspring to add to his line. When a kitten is included as payment, the date it is to be released to the stud's owner should be specified in the contract. Likewise, what type of inoculations the kitten will receive before release and at what age should be noted.

When the kittens are born the tom's owner is customarily notified right away, and if a kitten is to be transferred to the owner of the stud as partial or full payment he is kept informed of the kitten's progress regularly.

Very clear arrangements must be made beforehand covering the possibility that there might be a litter consisting of only one kitten or only one that survives the first few days. Usually the queen's owner has first claim to such a kitten.

Most breeder contracts provide for "return service." This covers the situation in which the queen is not impregnated during her first stay with the tom. Under a return service arrangement the female may be reshipped to the stud and re-bred to him at no additional charge.

If the owner of the queen keeps her indoors throughout the year, stipulation might be made that she not be bred in an outdoor mating cage, at least not in winter.

THE BREEDING PROCEDURE

When the female comes into season her owner will notify the owner of the stud. Almost always the female is sent to the male. She is usually mated several times while there and frequently spends a few days with the tom. The owner of the queen may accompany her. The stud's owner might prefer the queen's owner to stay away during the actual mating but often requests that the latter remain within calling distance.

Some breeders have a room at their cattery which is specifically set aside for mating. It is kept scrupulously clean, is peaceful and provides enough room for both male

Interior and exterior views of a very elaborate cattery. Not every new cat owner will go into the breeding of cats, but these photos show what a serious breeder's facilities might look like.

and female to socialize, breed and retire comfortably. Sometimes the breeding quarters are outdoors, but the same care and facilities are provided there as would be if they were inside.

Before being put together in the mating area the tom and the queen are usually placed in adjoining runs so that they can socialize. They get used to each other and their different cattery odors in this way and are therefore more relaxed when put together. The actual act of mating only lasts a minute or two, but when first together the cats may play or even sleep together. Oftentimes they will not mate until there are no humans present to watch them or not until after it is dark. They will be left together for several matings over a day or two and the queen will then go home.

Queening

PREPARATIONS

A pregnant female cat is called a queen. About sixty-four days after she has been successfully mated a litter can be expected. This gestation period can vary by a few days, but in general nine weeks is the rule. Mark your calendar and plan to stay home a few days before and after the sixty-fourth day. A few weeks before the kittens are due the queen should be introduced to the nestbox. The advantages of this are twofold; first, the chances of her having the babies in an inconvenient (for you) or dirty place are minimized, and second, because she has been accustomed to the kittening box beforehand, when the new mother delivers she will feel comfortable in the place you have chosen. If you do not provide a kittening box, it is not at all unlikely that your queen will deliver in your closet, under the sofa, on your bed or maybe even in a kitchen cabinet. For some people this wouldn't be bothersome, but others would find it unacceptable. If you decide that your cat should kitten in a place of your and not her choosing, remember that newborns are very adversely affected by direct sunlight which hurts their eyes and drafts and dampness which lead to colds and serious respiratory infections. For this reason it is not usually advisable to let your queen give birth in the cellar. Some breeders do indeed house their catteries in their cellars, but only after the cellars have been properly prepared for year-round comfort and protected from dampness, etc. Attics are usually too hot, and you won't want to be walking up and down the stairs too many times to look in on the kittens. Garages should not even be considered as suitable places for new families. An infant kitten is very weak, as is a human baby, and infancy is the most dangerous time of a cat's life since it is most susceptible to fatal disease at this time.

Perhaps the best place to put the kittening box is in one of your cat's favored spots, somewhere she tends to nap during the day. It's probably a place out of your home's mainstream of activity, quiet and indirectly lit. Of course some cats favor icebox tops or bookcases and these are obviously not good choices to place a nestbox. But even cats that favor high napping spots from where they can observe all that goes on below them often have a corner out of the way somewhere in which they sometimes relax; this is the ideal location for the kittening box. Remember to keep the room warm and draft-free as long as the kits are infants.

The nestbox should be lined with newspapers which keep the bottom warm and absorb moisture. These should be covered with an old sheet so that the newsprint does not rub off onto the fur. Your queen can get sick when she cleans herself or the kittens and ingests the newsprint ink. Blankets are not suggested as the kits have tiny, needle-like claws which can easily get tangled in the wool or acrylic nap. Old sheets on the other hand are smooth and soft. Color doesn't matter, although some people feel that white sheets, while allowing you to see the kits clearly against the stark white background, reflect too much light. If, however, the nestbox has been put in a place out of direct bright sunlight or strong desk lamps and the like, there should be no need to worry about light reflections from white sheets. The box should be long enough that your queen can stretch out comfortably and tall enough that infants can't easily wander over the walls.

After your queen is four or five weeks along, Vitamin A, Vitamin B and calcium supplements should be added to her diet. The diet itself should consist of the same good quality foods you normally feed her, foods rich in protein such as chicken, liver, heart, meat and eggs. Increased liquid intake before and after the birth of the kittens helps the mother produce enough milk.

Trimming the hair around your queen's nipples makes it

easier for the kits to suckle, but if your cat is not used to being held for nail clipping, brushing the stomach and the like, don't try this. Your queen could move suddenly, and if you are holding sharp-pointed scissors you could easily injure the mother or unborn kittens. It is always a good idea never to use sharp-pointed scissors on any animal. They are easily distracted and sudden movements can lead to accidents. Blunt, round-tipped scissors are always safer.

One last, very important point. A queen should be in familiar surroundings and with people she loves and trusts when she presents her kittens. To separate her from home and family at this crucial time puts unnecessary strain on her. While a boarding cattery or veterinarian's office may provide excellent facilities and care, neither can provide a new mother the love she is used to at home.

DELIVERY

As delivery time approaches your queen will spend much time in the box making a nest and getting settled. Your help will probably not be required, but you should be prepared to help and have on hand sterilized scissors and thread, warm but boiled water, a soft cloth, towel, heating pad or warm hot water bottle and paper and pencil. When she is ready to deliver her kittens the mother may inform you with a soft chirp or two. She may come and fetch you wherever you may be and get you to follow her back to the nest. Of course, she may choose not to inform you at all, and even if you are home when she gives birth she may be so quiet that you'll not be aware of this until after the fact.

Some understanding of how a cat fetus develops will be useful if you should have to assist during kittening. The fetus develops in a sac filled with liquid which is connected to the placenta, a disk of flesh attached to the uterine wall, by the umbilical cord. It is through this cord that nourishment reaches the fetus. During the birth process the muscles of the uterus contract to push the fetus in its sac down and out to the vaginal opening. Most kittens are born head-first, although sometimes they come feet-first (breech birth). There is no cause for alarm if there is a breech presentation unless your queen is particularly tiny or has had complications in the past. You may, however, be surprised the first time you see one.

Sometimes births are spread out over a few hours; this is a common occurrence. If contractions have continued for a long while but no kits have yet appeared, however, something is probably amiss and you should call your vet. When your queen is pushing the kits out but is having trouble, you may have to help. DON'T PUT YOUR FINGERS INTO THE VAGINA AND DON'T FORCE THE KITTEN OUT. MAKE SURE THAT YOUR HANDS ARE CLEAN. Use a towel to hold the sac after it has come out a bit. Do not pull the kitten; you are only holding it so that it doesn't slip back into the mother. With each contraction it will come out a bit more. After the kit is out, a little tug on the cord will bring out the placenta. Make sure there is one placenta for each kitten. When placenta material is left inside the mother it can become very dangerous to her health. If this has occurred, the vet should be called. After the kit has appeared, you should gently break the sac and, starting at the head, pull it back over the kitten. Cut the umbilical cord with your sterilized scissors about two inches from the baby's navel. Tie it off with the sterilized thread. The cord will dry up and fall off in a few days. If the kit fails to breathe, take it in a towel and rub. Breathing should begin right away. You can hold the infant upside down for a bit to clear its lungs.

Usually the kittens are born with the sac intact. The queen will tear the sac, bite through the cord and eat the sac, cord and placenta. When kits are delivered quickly in succession the mother may not have time to do this and you should remove sacs etc. as unobtrusively as possible. The mother will lick the newborns dry. There will often be a lot of mewing and squealing as the little ones often exercise their voices immediately. After all of the kits have been born, the queen will clean herself, count noses and attend to her babies. You can give the mother some warm milk or favored food at this time as she may be hungry or thirsty. Clean sheets can be added and dirty materials removed from the box a little while after delivery. A normal litter consists of about four kittens, but don't be surprised if there's only one or as many as ten.

AFTERCARE

Your queen may choose not to sleep with the newborns. If this happens you will have to provide warmth for them with a heating pad or warm hot water bottle. Be careful that the temperature you provide is not too hot; too much heat can burn the kits' tender skin or dehydrate them. Set the heating pad at its lowest setting and cover it with a sheet folded over several times. Remember not to leave the heating pad too long; the heat buildup could be dangerous. A warm hot water bottle is safer, but the water will have to be changed frequently. During the night the bottle should be used rather than the pad. Most mothers will spend time in the box with their family, and the above information is provided in the event you have one of those mother cats that spends no time in the box other than to feed the babies.

Mothers lick the anal region of their babies to encourage elimination. She then eats the wastes. If your queen fails to care for her kittens in this way you can use soft wetted cotton to rub the kit's tummy and anus to stimulate excretion. You will have to clean up the liquid and solid waste matter. Diarrhea in little kittens is usually symptomatic of something more serious. If you notice this call your veterinarian for advice. He will probably suggest you bring a waste sample for him to look at. Prompt attention is important lest the kitten become dehydrated.

Newborns do nothing but sleep, eat and eliminate for the

first days. They get all their nourishment from their mother's milk which is a complete food. For this reason the mother's diet should continue to be enriched as it was before she kittened. If you notice that some of the babies appear weaker than others, put the weaker ones on the rear nipples.

After a while you may notice a small lump over a kitten's navel which indicates that it has failed to heal properly and a hernia has developed. This may or may not be dangerous, and your vet should be consulted.

Around the fourth week you will notice that the babies are no longer infants. They will have opened their eyes and they will leave the box regularly. Soon they become accustomed to food other than mother's milk. You can introduce them to adult cat food by putting some on your finger and allowing them to lick it off. Strained or junior meat human baby food is often enjoyed by kittens, and adult cats appreciate it as well. At a cost of almost fifty cents per jar, however, it is rather expensive. The kittens are often introduced to adult cat food when they are first exposed to their mother's dinner. After they have stepped in the food and cleaned off their paws, they often go back for more. Many persons recommend not feeding tuna at this time as it may be hard for the kittens to digest. The babies are usually weaned by six weeks.

The kits no longer spend much time in the box except perhaps to sleep there. Your queen may have long since moved her litter to a place more of her choosing than the kittening box. Since she has given in to your wishes once by having the babies in a place of your choosing, the kittening box, at this time you will probably fight a losing battle with her when you replace the kittens to the box. At her first convenience the mother will again move the litter. So acquiesce to her demands and call it a draw. There is one place you should not allow the queen to house the babies and this is the litter box. Some time after the kittens' eyes have opened they will learn to use the litter box by observing the mother. It is unsanitary and dangerous to allow them to sleep where they excrete their wastes. It is usually not too difficult to break the mother's will in this instance. If, however, the mother has moved her family out of the nest box and into the litter box before about 4 weeks, the blind kits will often stuff their mouths with the kitty litter granules since they are unaware of the litter's true purpose.

When the kittens first spend a lot of time out of the nest running around, exploring and napping, they are not used to your big feet and your big behind, so be more observant than normal about where you step and sit. Soon the kits will move out of the way of your feet, but you still will have to look before you sit when the kittens are tiny. Much of the earliest time out of the box will be spent following mother around, but there's usually at least one kitten that ventures out on its own a lot. And yes, even if you open a closet or under-the-sink cupboard for only a moment, the curious will often make their way inside without you ever noticing. You may have to make a nose-count occasionally, and this is always a good idea at feeding time, before you go to sleep, or before you leave the house for any reason.

After four weeks is the best time to get the kittens used to being petted and handled. You were probably able to touch the youngsters earlier than this, but perhaps the mother cat had indicated that this displeased her. In any case, now that the children can see you, the pleasing sound of your voice which was their first introduction to you, the feel of your hand and the visual image of you should soon represent something pleasurable to them. They may be shy at first, but because they observe their mother so frequently they will see her with you and hear her contented purring, and will soon imitate her behavior with you. The kittens' temperaments are developing at this time and pleasurable encounters will leave lasting impressions on the young animals. Sudden movements and aggressive behavior toward the kittens should be avoided. They enjoy play but not threats or ill-handling.

By watching the litter as it develops, you can observe the individual personalities of the kittens. You will notice which kitten always recognizes your voice, which one learns the use of the litter box faster than the others, which gets used to solid food early, which is lazy, which is active, which is affectionate, which is curious and which is independent. At eight weeks you should have already decided how many of the kittens you intend to keep and how many are going to new homes.

Which you choose one day may not be the same you choose the next day, but after a few days a firm decision should be reached that won't be regretted later. If you decide later on to become a serious breeder, the choice is made easier in that prospective breeder, show and pet animals can be selected more easily by the experienced eye.

If there are small children at home, they should be taught how to properly pick up and hold a young kitten. Let them start while sitting on the floor so that if the kitten falls it will not be hurt. Impress upon youngsters that cats do not like to be hit or wrestled with and are especially annoyed by tail-pulling. When your child is scratched by your cat you can be sure that the child is at fault. A cat will invariably warn you with growls and postures that it doesn't appreciate particular handling and almost always strikes out in retaliation rather than aggression.

Kittens usually receive their first vaccinations before they are twelve weeks old; booster shots are usually given after this, after they are weaned. Your vet will suggest the proper times and types of protection which are best for your particular cat. Remember that after the kittens are weaned they no longer receive antibodies from their mother in her milk; inoculations are therefore a necessity for their well-being.

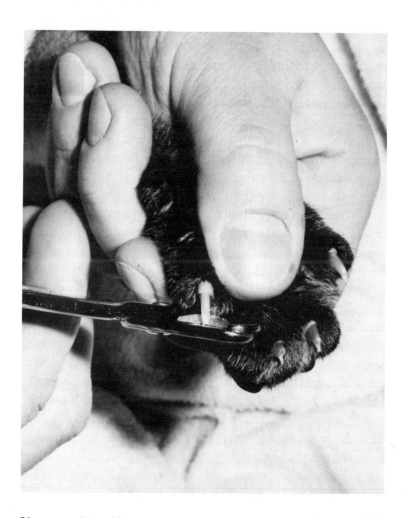

Since newborn kittens are so delicate, they can easily be inadvertently hurt by their mother's claws if these have not been trimmed a few days before the anticipated delivery date of the babies. Regular clipping of your cat's claws is a must all the time. Your pet will not get caught in the rug or furniture, in your clothing when in your arms or in your lap and will not suffer from ingrown or backgrown claws if you conscientiously attend to them. In each claw you will be able to see a thin red line extending toward the tip. This is the blood vessel which serves the claw. Be very careful not to cut into this as it is most painful to your cat when you do. If you trim the claws once a week (and as a responsible cat owner you will of course) it will only be necessary to trim off the pointed tip of each claw. Photo by the author with another "thank you" to Cathy and Nicholas Rocat.

Under no circumstances should you allow kittens outdoors or to another household until they have been properly protected against disease. Sometime around ten or twelve weeks of age the kittens are ready to go to their new homes.

If you have the father cat as well as the mother you will probably notice that he doesn't involve himself too much with the kittens for the first few weeks. Occasionally he will come over to the box and watch a while, but rare is the father that spells the mother in the nest. After the little ones' eyes have opened and they start to venture from the nest, their father will delight in playing with them. It may seem that he gets too rough at times, but you'll notice that the little ones keep coming back for more. If he should tire of games before the little ones do, he will more than likely retire to a napping spot high up where the kits can't get to him. Mother cats also use this tactic when they want to be left alone. Sometimes it does happen that father cats will harm the babies but this appears to be quite rare. You'll know if something is awry as the mother will come to the defense of the babies and after a little fur flies both mother and father will preen themselves and retire for a nap. When this has occurred, however, it is best to segregate the father from the rest of the family.

If you have chosen to breed your female and plan on continuing to do so, be responsible. There are so many cats and kittens needlessly put down every day because homes could not be found for them. The sick feeling you will get giving your unwanted kittens away to a shelter is terrible. Find homes for your kittens, preferably before you mate your queen. When you become aware of the time and effort it takes to responsibly breed cats you may no longer wish to get involved in it. Cats that will not be bred should be neutered so that they don't suffer breeding pangs. They might become more affectionate, certainly not less so, and they'll be happier, calmer and healthier.

Ch. Jonlyn's Mandy of Ming-Tai, Chocolate Point female bred by John and Jacqueline Grant and owned by Ruth Zimmermann. 1. Mandy a few days before she was due to deliver. 2. Mandy in delivery cage one day before her kittens were born. The cage has been placed on a table and put at the foot of her owner's bed so that the owner can assist quickly if necessary. Many breeders feel that their queens are happiest and most comfortable when they are near to their humans at the time of delivery. Confinement to a delivery cage provides maximum safety for the newborns and the queen. Oftentimes the stud will be close at hand to watch and talk to his mate. Photos by Ruth Zimmermann.

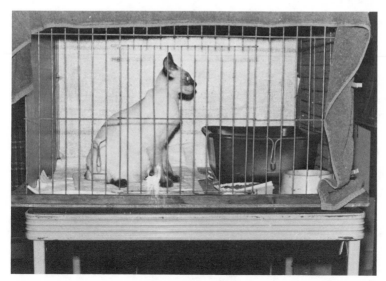

1. The first kitten is being delivered in a breech (feet first) presentation. The kitten's head is not yet presented and she is still enveloped in the birth sac. 2. The queen is cleaning off her first-born. All photos on these pages by Ruth Zimmermann.

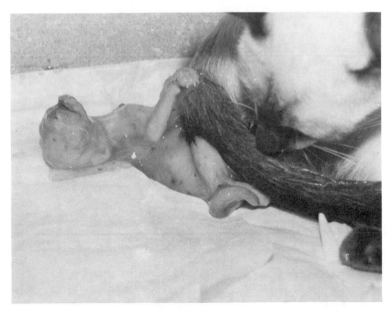

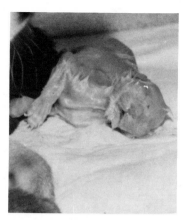

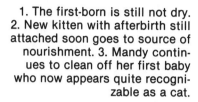

1. The first-born is still not dry. 2. New kitten with afterbirth still attached soon goes to source of nourishment. 3. Mandy continues to clean off her first baby who now appears quite recognizable as a cat.

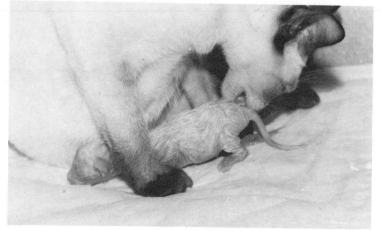

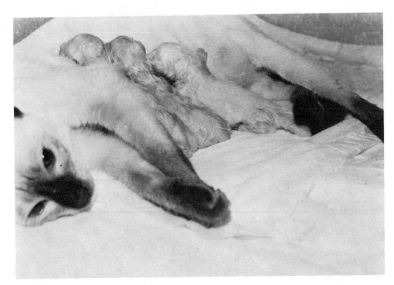

1. Mother has removed afterbirth and washed both children. Kittens feed while mother rests awaiting next delivery. 2. Third and last kitten has been born, washed and dried. All three kittens feed while queen purrs and rests. This is the time for you to offer your new mother a favored treat as she may be quite hungry at this time. 3. Four-day old kittens. It will be a few days before the characteristic Siamese points begin to be noticeable. 4. Mother with three-day old family. All photos by Ruth Zimmermann.

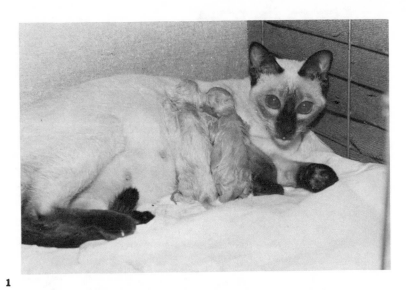

3

4

Siamese Varieties

The first Siamese brought to Europe and North America were frequently cross-eyed, often had kinks in their thick heavy tails, were domestic bodied and round- or "apple-" headed. Today's Siamese is no longer cross-eyed, has a long, thin, unkinked and tapering tail, a tapered wedge-shaped head and a foreign (medium in size, dainty, long and svelte) body. Only the color of the eyes (blue) and the distinctive color pattern of the body and extremities link the Siamese of yesterday with the Siamese of today.

Siamese have a body of one color and "points" (tail, feet, ears and face) of another. The color of the points distinguishes the varieties of the breed and gives them their names. Thus, one refers to Seal Point Siamese, Seal Points or Seals, Red Point Siamese, Red Points or Reds and so on.

There is much disagreement among Siamese breeders and exhibitors over the acceptability of certain point and pattern colors in the breed. Some hold that only Seal, Blue, Chocolate and Frost Points are true Siamese while others recognize Tabby, Tortie, Red, Cream, Tortie/Tabby and Albino varieties as well. Because of this dispute, Siamese with points of any of the colors last mentioned are also known as Colorpoint Shorthairs.

Despite any artificial nomenclature, all of the above are equally recognizable as Siamese by almost anyone who sees them. A detailed discussion of the arguments proposed by the parties concerned and involved in the color controversy is beyond the scope of this book. For those who are in-

Rocat's Copper Penny of Dei-Jai climbing down from the kitten cage to investigate the surroundings—curiosity is a characteristic of all domesticated cats and perhaps one of their greatest charms. Photo by the author.

terested in pursuing this subject further, the national breed clubs of the various registering organizations should be able to provide or at least lead one to further information.

Tyrone, handsome two-year-old Seal Point male belonging to Janice Lees, sitting by the door while waiting to be allowed back into the house. Photo by the author.

Seal Points are what many people have in mind when they think of Siamese cats. They were the first variety to be brought to Europe and America and have through the years remained the most popular. For a while the breed was known as the Royal Cat of Siam because it had been, reputedly, a favorite of the Siamese royal family. For this reason one occasionally hears Seals called Royals or Royal Points by veteran cat fanciers, or encounters the term in older books dealing with the breed. Seals are often considered the "natural" or "foundation" variety of Siamese since the Blue, Chocolate and, as a dilute of Blue, Lilac varieties result after modification of the seal (black) color.

Blues were for some time considered poor-quality Seals. They began to gain acceptance after a while, however, and at shows they competed against Seals in the Siamese division. In 1932 the Boston Cat Club Show became the first in America to judge a separate class for Blues.

A Blue Point male, Tempura's Yours Truly, became, in 1956, the first Siamese of any variety to win the *Cats Magazine* Cat of the Year Award.

Two major theories have been proposed to explain the development of Blue Point Siamese. The first suggests that since blue color is a dilute of black, it is certainly possible that color-diluted offspring (Blues) could, occasionally, be naturally produced by black (Seal) parents. Seals with no Blue or Blue-carrying traceable ancestors sometimes produce a Blue kitten even today, and this is after many, many years of selective breeding in their lines.

The second theory holds that matings in the wild between Seal Point Siamese and silver-blue Korats produced offspring that carried both color factors. Subsequent offspring could have, in turn, appeared as Seal Point Siamese, Korats and Blue Point Siamese. This theory, however, remains conjecture as no one has reported publicly the results of a detailed breeding program between the two breeds mentioned.

A fine litter of Dei-Jai kittens at six weeks old. Center is a Seal and the others are Chocolates by Ch. Dei-Jai's Ar-Kai x Ch. Dei-Jai's Angelic Imp. Photo by the author.

The history of the Chocolates parallels that of the Blues. Considered inferior Seals, early Chocolates were often neutered, were regularly disqualified or prevented from competing at shows and were scorned by Siamese breeders and exhibitors. The breeding of Chocolate Points did not receive serious attention until after WW II when Brian Stirling-Webb, a noted British fancier, helped to establish the color. GCCF recognized the variety in 1950, and several U.S. associations followed suit over the next few years.

Since chocolate or light brown is a diluted form of black, offspring of this color could, in Nature, be produced by

Seal parents just as Blues could. Matings in the wild between Seal Points and self-brown cats of which we have no record could produce offspring whose subsequent matings would produce Seal Point Siamese, Chocolate Point Siamese and self-browns.

Chocolate Points do not always breed true and Lilacs occasionally appear in Chocolate litters.

In this photo of Dei-Jai cats asleep together are Seal, Chocolate and Blue Point Siamese and a Chestnut and a Tortie Oriental Shorthair. Photo by the author.

Lilacs or Frosts are dilutes that first began to appear in Blue litters in North America in the early 1950s. By 1954 they had been recognized by ACA and CFF and became, therefore, the first Siamese variety to be recognized in America before it was in Britain. No Lilacs, in fact, were even born in Britain until 1955. Although Lilacs were originally bred from cats which had both Chocolate and Blue in their ancestry, the lilac color of the points, like the chocolate of the Chocolates but unlike the blue of the Blues, does not tend to spread to the coat.

The first serious efforts to develop new Siamese varieties were made in the late 1940s. Many fanciers, on both sides of the Atlantic, opposed these attempts and held that a new breed was being developed rather than new varieties of an established breed. Eventually the new varieties were accepted by some as just that while others classified them as a new breed which came to be known, in America, as Colorpoint Shorthair. In Britain, the new color varieties were

Make sure your cat's toys are not made from or do not contain harmful substances. The cloth mouse this kitten is playing with is a fine toy. Rocat's Copper Penny of Dei-Jai a little older than he was in the photo in which he's climbing down from the kitten cage. Red Point Siamese like Penny are known in some associations as Colorpoint Shorthairs. Photo by the author.

Blue and Seal Point kittens at six weeks of age. Photo by the author.

classified as "Siamese, Any Other Colour." "Other," of course, referred to any color other than seal, blue, chocolate or lilac.

Red Points were produced by breeding Seal Points with self-red or red tabby Shorthairs and then mating the resulting offspring with Siamese. In the later 1930s Dr. Joseph C. Thompson of San Francisco became interested and involved in the development of Reds. From the 1940s on Alyce de Filippe advocated the acceptance and worked on the development of Red Points and it is Mrs. de Filippe who is most directly responsible for the success of this variety in the United States. Because of the likelihood of producing cats that are red or tabby all over, Red Points are sometimes bred with Seals to keep the correct color contrast between the points and body.

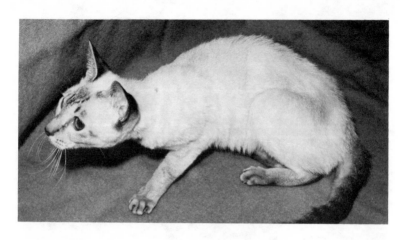

1. Fefe's Tessa Lee of Rocat, Chocolate Lynx Point female. In some associations Lynx are registered not as Siamese but as Colorpoint Shorthairs. 2. Sometimes photographing kittens yields very satisfactory results. The use of a prop is most helpful to contain and restrict your subject. Six-week old Blue Point kitten bred and owned by Janice Lees. Both photos by the author.

Creams first appeared in litters with Reds after that variety began to be seriously bred. This is only proper since cream is a simple dilute of red. It has been suggested that some Creams were produced by breeding Red Points to self-cream shorthairs and then breeding the resulting offspring back to Reds. ACFA accepted the variety in 1979.

Tabby (Lynx) Point Siamese were created when tabbies were used in Red Point breeding programs in the 1940s. Early on the Lynx were called Silver Points. It is interesting to note, however, that Tabby Points were included among "Any Other Colour" Siamese in Frances Simpson's famous 1902 work *The Book Of The Cat.*

Tortie (Tortoiseshell) Points were, like Lynx, produced when Reds were bred. Crossing Lynx and Torties results in Tortie/Lynx Points. Torties and Lynxes were recognized by ACFA in 1966.

A rarely seen variety of Siamese is the Albino which has a white coat, pink skin and a pink undertone in the eyes.

2

American Cat Fanciers Association (ACFA) Siamese Standard Of Perfection

SCALE OF POINTS

HEAD   15
Profile 5
Wedge 6
Chin 4
EARS   7
Size 4
Set 3
EYE SHAPE   8
EYE COLOR   8
Color 5
Brilliance 3
BODY TYPE   10
NECK   3
Length 2
Carriage 1
LEGS AND FEET   7
Length and Boning of Leg 4
Shape and Size of Feet 3
TAIL   6
Length 4
Narrow at Base 1
Taper 1
COAT   8
Closeness, Texture 4
Shortness 4
BODY COLOR   8
Tone and Depth of Color 4
Shadings 4

Fan-C Love Is Blue held aloft by CFA judge Donna Davis after winning "Best Cat" under Davis at the Virginia Beach Cat Fanciers Show in 1979. This beautiful Blue Point was sired by Singa Mikado of Fan-C x Fan-C Blue Danube. She was bred and is owned by Barbara Baylor.

98

POINTS 10
Depth and Evenness 4
Pattern 4
Leather 2
CONDITION 5
BALANCE 5
Overall Appearance 3
Amenability 2
TOTAL 100

SIAMESE COLORS

CHOCOLATE POINT — The body color of a Chocolate Point Siamese should be an ivory color all over, shading if at all to be in the color of the points. The points should be a warm milk chocolate color, the ears, mask, legs, paws and tail to be as even in color as possible. Allowance should be made for incomplete mask, etc., in kittens and younger cats. The ears should not be darker than the other points. As a result of diluted pigmentation of the points, the flesh tones show through at the tip of the nose leather, resulting in a burnt rose tone, while the foot pads have a salmon pink color. Eyes should be a brilliant blue, deeper tones preferred.

Objections: Exhibits with dark intensity of tone or foot pads and the tip of the nose leather, as seen in the Seal Point Siamese, shall be disqualified for competition in the Chocolate Point class.

BLUE POINT — The body of the Blue Point Siamese should be an even platinum gray of bluish tones, shading gradually into a lighter color on the belly and chest. Points should be a deeper grayish-blue tone, all points being as nearly the same shade as possible. Flesh tones of nose leather and foot pads to be a dark blue-gray. Eyes should be a brilliant blue, deeper tones preferred.

Objections: Fawn or cream shadings. Foot pads or nose leather in any light shade including flesh pink or a lilac hue shall disqualify exhibit for competition in the Blue Point Classes.

99

SEAL POINT — The body color of the Seal Point Siamese should be an even pale fawn or cream, shading gradually into a lighter color on the belly and chest. Points should be dense, deep seal brown, all points being of the same shade. Eyes brilliant blue, deeper shades preferred. Flesh tones of nose leather and foot pads to be a dark brown, almost black in color.

Objections: Black or gray shadings. Foot pads or nose leather in any light shade including flesh, salmon pink or burnt rose shall disqualify exhibit for competition in the Seal Point classes.

Very lovely young Seal kitten with points developing very nicely. This purr-sonality plus kitten was bred by Catherine Rowan. Photo by the author.

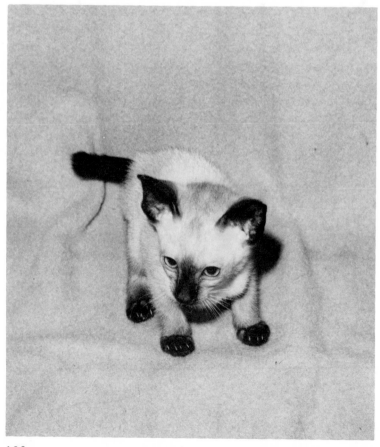

Very typey Seal Point female, Oldwick Deirdre of Rocat at four years old by Chuhulainn x Ch. Siobohn Sweetums; breeder: Everett J. Landers; owner: Catherine Rowan. Photo by the author.

101

Very pretty Blue Point female, Fefe's Libby Mae of Rocat at nine months. Libby was bred by Laurie L. Sarno and is owned by Catherine Rowan.

RED POINT—The body of the Red Point Siamese should be a warm even, creamy white, shading if any, the same tone as points. The points should be a deep orange red, a "hot" color, the deeper the better. Since red is a slowly developing color, two years should be allowed for full point color intensity to develop. Kittens should be white in body with hot cream points. Absence of barring desirable. Foot pads and nose leather to be hot pink. Eyes should be a brilliant blue, deeper shades preferred.

Objections: Black or blue flecks in nose leather or foot pads, black or cream patches on body or point color, showing even slight Torti pattern shall be a disqualification from the Red Point class. Any pale tone, overall impression of overall color to be "hot."

FROST POINT — The body color of the Frost Point Siamese should be an even milk white color shading, if any, in the color of the points. The points should be a frosty gray of pinkish tone, the dilute pigment permitting the flesh tone to show through,

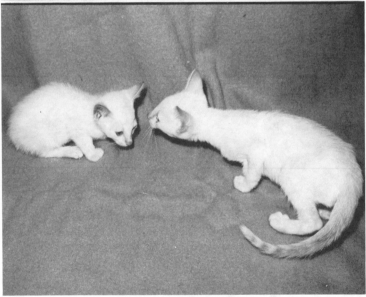

While Copper Penny (right) and his smaller litter brother were playing, Libby (right) and Laurie (domestic shorthair, left) watched with extreme interest. You'll soon learn that your Siamese wants to know everything that's going on in the house and will probably be right in the middle of the activity before long. Photos by the author.

resulting in a delicate peach blossom tone of the inner surface of the ears, while the foot pads have a coral pink color, and the nose leather presents a translucent old lilac hue at the tip. The eyes should be brilliant blue, the deeper shade preferred.

Objections: Exhibits with dark intensity of tone of foot pads and tip of the nose leather, as seen in Blue Point Siamese, shall be disqualified for competition in the Frost Point classes.

Int. Ch., Dbl. Gr. Ch. and Tr. Ch. Kris Kringle of Ming-Tai, AE, AA, POP 1974, 1975, 1976, Lilac Point male at two years of age. A very impressive cat. Photo by Paul Stankus courtesy of Ruth Zimmermann.

Fefe's Tessa Lee of Rocat, Chocolate Lynx Point female at three and a half years old. Tessa was sired by Sanan Nam's Billie The Kid of Fefe (Seal Point) x Mandi's Velvet Joy of Fefe (Blue Lynx) and was bred by Laurie L. Sarno. She is beautifully marked which can be seen in the photo and is a delight to handle . Photo by the author.

CREAM POINT—The body of the Cream Point Siamese is to be an even white all over, shading, if any, to be same color as points. Points may be any shade of cream from a deep almost red to a pale cream. The overall impression to be a dull color as opposed to the hot tone of the red point. On deeper specimens the impression will be a deep almost red color with a dull bluish overtone. On paler specimens the impression will be a very pale reddish tone with a frosted overtone.

Objections: Hot point color. Specimens showing hot Red Point color to be transferred to Red Point classes.

LYNX POINT — Body and point color same as above. The body color to be clear without visible stripes preferred. Shading if any to be in the same tones as point color. Allowance made for slow development of color and stripes on Chocolate, Frost and Red Lynx Point kittens and young cats. Frost is especially slow to develop color. Overall appearance of the dilutes, even when mature, will be pale. The mask to be in point color shading. Definite vertical stripes on the forehead, horizontal stripes from corners of the eye over the cheeks. Dark spots on whisker pads at base of whiskers and dark spot on either side of nose. Light spot at inner corner below eye is normal. Chin pale. Nose leather to be pink or conforming to recognized Siamese standard for point color with outer edges lined in point color. Some pink in nose leather preferred, but an otherwise outstanding specimen should not be penalized for lack of pink color. Front part of nose bridge fawn on Seals and Chocolates, silver-gray on Blues and Frosts, orange-red on Reds. Ears to be solid color, depending on point color, with paler thumb mark. Outer edges lined in lighter color. Thumb mark less distinct on Blues and Frosts. The legs to be a light shade, depending on point color, with distinct dark point color on back of legs (hocks) and webbing between toes. Bars of light point color on legs to hips and shoulders where bars fade into shading. Paw pads to correspond with point color. The tail should have definite stripes of point color on light background tipped with dark point color. Eyes of brilliant blue, deeper shades preferred, with point color lining.

Objections: Hood over head; bars on body; improper pad colors; gray tones on Seals and Chocolates, brown tones on Blues and Frosts, patching on Reds; pale eye color.

TORTIE/LYNX POINT — Same as Lynx Point with the following exceptions: Ears: mottled; Nose and pad leather: mottled; Tail: as above but mottling usually present; Points: patched with red and/or cream over tabby pattern.

TORTIE POINT — Standard same as above with the following exceptions. Seal, chocolate, blue, frost, clear shading on body if present to be in same tone as points. It must be noted that body shading on Torti Points will be mottled. Allowance to be made for slow development of color on Chocolate and Frost kittens and on young cats. The ears, mask, tail and legs should show definite red or cream mottling. While a blaze is desirable, the absence of one should not be penalized providing the mask is well mottled and attractive. It must be remembered that, as in all Siamese, type must be considered more important than minor

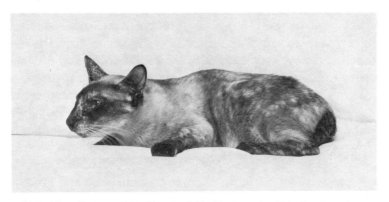

A.M.P. Kara Grace of Rocat, Seal Tortie female. Kara's parents are Altair's Mickey of A.M.P. x Dbl. Ch. A.M.P.'s Queen Lizz and her breeder is Anna M. Pauch. Tortie Siamese are recognized only as Tortie Colorpoints in some association. Kara is very nicely marked and shows off well the Seal Tortoiseshell pattern. She is also the mother of little Copper Penny. Photo by the author.

color imperfections. Leather of nose and pads to conform to recognized Siamese standard for point color except where blaze or mottling extend into leather giving a spotted effect. The eyes should be a dark brilliant blue.

Objections: Absence of any mottling in ears or tail; white toes or definite patches or white as in calico.

SEAL TORTIE POINT — The body color of the Seal Tortie Point should be pale fawn or cream in color, mottled in older cats, shading gradually into a lighter color on the belly and chest. Points should be uniformly mottled seal-brown and red or cream. Ears and tail should show red or cream and seal brown mottling. Allowance should be made for lack of red in kittens and young cats as the color is very slow to develop. The mask should show some mottling and a blaze is desirable. The nose leather should be dark brown, almost black, except where the blaze extends into the leather. Foot pads should also show dark brown with pink patches where the mottling extends into the paw pads. Eyes should be a dark, brilliant blue, even approaching violet.

Objections: Tortie points showing only two colors instead of three. White toes (meaning a half moon over all four toes, not an individual white toe) or definite white patches as in calico.

107

1. Ch. Jonlyn's Mandy of Ming-Tai. We met Mandy earlier giving birth to her kittens. A toy like the wooden clothespin Mandy is playing with is fine as she cannot hurt herself with it. Don't leave things like cigarette butts, matches, pins, needles and the like about as they can only cause trouble. 2. Seal Point male, Ch. Jonlyn's Pinocchio of Ming-Tai. "J.P." is the father of Mandy's kittens. Both cats bred by John and Jacqueline Grant and both are owned by Ruth Zimmermann. Photos by Ruth Zimmermann.

FROST TORTIE POINT — The body of the Frost Tortie Point should be milk white, mottling if any in the shade of the points. Cream mottling should show faintly in the ears and tail, mask and points. Again a blaze is desirable. The foot pads, basically a coral pink should show lighter pink spots. The nose leather, old lilac in hue, will show pink spots if the blaze is present. The Frost Tortie Point will be very slow to develop color and the overall appearance, even when mature, will be pale.

Objections: Absence of any mottling in ears or tail. White toes (see Seal Tortie Point) or white patches as in calico.

CHOCOLATE TORTIE POINT — The body color should be an ivory color all over, mottled in older cats. The points should be a warm milk chocolate and cream or red mottled. Ears and tail should show definite red or cream mottling. The mask should also show some mottling and a blaze is desirable. Foot pads should be salmon pink in color showing lighter spots where the mottling has extended into the pads. Nose leather should be burnt rose in tone except where the blaze extends into it. Eyes should be a dark, brilliant blue, even approaching violet.

Objections: Exhibits with dark intensity of tone on foot pads or nose leather as seen in Seal Points. White toes (see Seal Tortie Point) or definite white patches as in calico.

BLUE TORTIE POINT—The body of the Blue Tortie Point should be a mottled platinum gray of bluish tones and cream shading to a lighter tone on the chest and belly. Mottling may be absent in young cats and kittens in the body coat. Points should be a deeper blue-gray mottled with red or cream. The mask should also have red or cream mottling and the blaze is desired. Ears and tail should show definite red and cream mottling in the blue-gray color. Nose leather may show a pink spot on the normally dark blue-gray if a blaze is present. Footpads to be dark blue-gray with light pink mottling. Eyes to be a dark, brilliant blue, almost violet.

Objections: White toes (see Seal Tortie Point) or definite white patches as in calico.

Poor Nicholas. Earlier you saw him having his ears cleaned, claws clipped, eyes cleaned and being given a pill; now a bath. 1. Before wetting your cat make sure the water is comfortable against the inside of your wrist. Have something in the sink or bathtub that your cat can grip with its feet so it doesn't slide all over. Maintaining a firm grip, wet your cat away from his head. 2. Apply soap taking care not to get any in your cat's eyes. 3. Work up a rich lather in your cat's coat. This is not the time to let go of your grip so don't forget to hold on. 4. Rinse thoroughly; don't squirt the cat in the ears and certainly not in the face. 5. Towel dry vigorously; your pet will enjoy this anyway, but it's important so that he doesn't get chilled. 6. After drying with a towel, brush the coat and air-dry. It may take a while before your cat is accustomed to the noise of the electric dryer. 7. Sleek down the dry coat, give words of encouragement and Puss can leave and regain his dignity. All photos by the author.

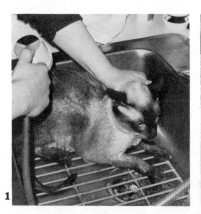

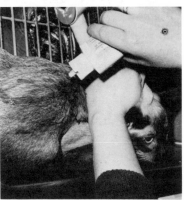

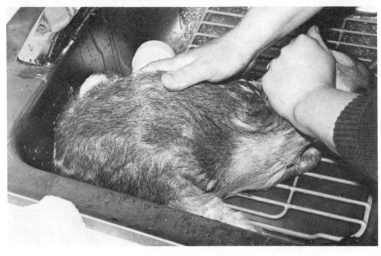

4

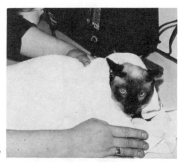

5

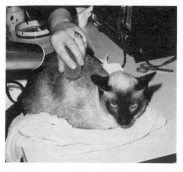

6

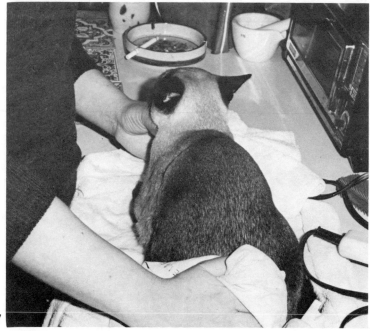

7

Ch. D'Purr Toreador of LuBo, Blue Point Himalayan male. Sire: War-jo's Prince Valiant of D'Purr; dam: Ch. Contiss Honeysuckle of D'Purr. Toreador was bred by Dea Jumper and is owned by A. Louis Zimmer-Vafiadis. Those who admired the coloring of the Siamese and the long hair and body type of the Persian began to crossbreed the two breeds in order to produce a Persian type cat with Siamese markings. The Himalayan is the man-made cat that resulted from these crossbreedings first seriously carried out in the 1920s. Himalayans come in all the colors that Siamese do as well as solid brown, solid lilac, lilaccream and bluecream. While not as popular as the Siamese, the Himalayan has recently passed the Persian to become America's second most popular purebred cat. Photo by the author.

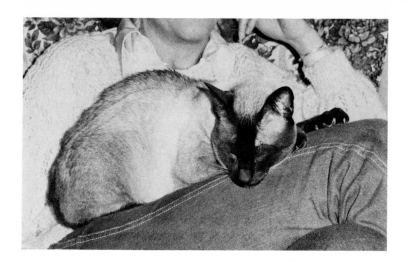

Tyrone asleep on his master's lap. Most people feel that cats are aloof and stand-offish. They are, rather, very choosy about whom they will accept. When a cat trusts you enough to take a nap in your lap, you have measured up to a cat's very demanding standards of acceptance. Photo by the author.

On the following pages are two breeds related to the Siamese. All self- (solid-) colored Siamese type cats are known in the United States as Oriental Shorthairs. They were developed when English breeders began to produce a solid-colored brown cat without tabby markings. These cats came to be known as Havanas and Chestnut Orientals; they were developed by crossing Chocolate Siamese with Russian Blues or with black domestics.

During the Second World War breeding cats was obviously difficult. The Russian Blue was particularly hard hit and following the war Blue Point Siamese were used in Russian Blue breeding programs. There were two reasons for this: because there were so few Russian Blue stud males available suitable substitutes had to be found; additionally, breeders began to become interested in refining the type of the Russian Blue. The Siamese was a logical choice to use in these postwar breeding programs because a blue variety existed in the breed and the breed possessed a type compatible with that of the Russian Blue. Today, of course, crossbreeding Russian Blues and Siamese is frowned upon, but the historical fact exists that many of today's Russian Blues do in fact have Siamese ancestry somewhere in the back of their pedigrees.

113

2

1. Dei-Jai Statuette of Diadem ("Minx") a fifteen-month-old Chestnut Oriental Shorthair bred by Doris and Bill Thoms and owned by Anne Reichle. The distinctive Siamese type is clearly visible in this photo by the author.
2. The exquisite female Russian Blue Ch. Nordic Ingrid Joy of Rocat. Ingrid's parents are Gr. Ch. Nordic Blue Chip x Ch. Three Crown Blue Print of Nordic; she was bred by Natalie del Vecchio and is owned by Catherine Rowan. Photo by the author.

Siamese have a lot of energy and often like to rough-house it. A good companion housecat for a Siamese is another Siamese or a cat of a breed with the stamina of the Siamese. Some good choices include the Oriental Shorthair, Egyptian Mau or American Shorthair. Pictured: Fefe's Libby Mae of Rocat, Blue Point Siamese, and Rocat's Miss Molly, Bronze Egyptian Mau. Both photos by the author.

Useful Addresses

Registering Associations

ACA (American Cat Association). Mrs. Lois Foster, Box 533, Georgetown, Florida 32039.

ACFA (American Cat Fanciers Association). Cora Swan, Kathy Snowden, P.O. Box 203, Point Lookout, Missouri 65726.

CCA (Canadian Cat Association). Nelson Street West, Suite 5, Brampton, Ontario, Canada.

CFA (Cat Fanciers Association). Jean Rose, P.O. Box 430, Red Bank, New Jersey 07701.

CFF (Cat Fanciers Federation). Grace Clute, 2013 Elizabeth Street, Schenectady, New York 12303.

TICA (The International Cat Association). Bob Mullen, 211 East Olive, Suite 201, Burbank, California 91502.

UCF (United Cat Federation). Jean Ford, 6616 East Hereford Drive, Los Angeles, California 90022.

Overleaf: Left is Vi-Lyn Melody, a Seal Point Himalayan bred by Mrs. E. Boguszewski and owned by Barbara and Donald Dulberg. This pretty lady is over ten years old! When cat fanciers wanted a longhaired cat with Siamese color pattern, they crossbred Siamese with Persians, and after much work produced the "Himmy." The Balinese, right, the true longhair Siamese, is a natural mutation, while the Himalayan was produced by man through deliberate crosses between two existing breeds. Only in the past decade or so have the beautiful Balis been regularly exhibited at shows, but as more have been seen, the breed has become increasingly popular. Balinese come in all the varieties that Siamese do, but some associations refer to certain color varieties as Javanese.

Five beautiful Siamese and Oriental Shorthair Dei-jai kittens from several litters bred by Doris and Bill Thoms. Pictured (all at six weeks old) are two Chocolate Point Siamese, one Seal Point Siamese and two Chestnut Oriental Shorthairs. Photo by the author.

Breed Clubs

Siamese Cat Society of America. Susie Page, President, 10065 Foothill Blvd., Lake View Terrace, California 91342.

Balinese Breeders and Fanciers of America. Diana Price, 1353 Forest Avenue, Carlsbad, California 92008.

International Himalayan Society. Larry Keely, 11751 Ranchito Street, El Monte, California 91732.

The Himalayan Society. Judy Sporer, R.D. 1, Mohawk, New York 13407.

Other Organizations

Morris Animal Foundation. 45 Inverness Drive East, Englewood, Colorado 80112.

S.O.C.K. (Save Our Cats & Kittens) Corp. 794 Hawthorne Drive, Walnut Creek, California 94596.

120

Bibliography

SIAMESE TITLES
Eustace, May. *100 Years Of Siamese Cats.* New York: Charles Scribner's Sons, 1978.

Lauder Phyllis. *The Batsford Book Of The Siamese Cat.* Philadelphia/New York: J.B. Lippincott Company, 1974.

Lauder, Phyllis. *The Siamese Cat.* Revised Edition. New York: Charles Scribner's Sons, 1979.

Naples, Marge. *This Is The Siamese Cat.* Second Edition, revised and expanded. Neptune, New Jersey: T.F.H. Publications, Inc. 1978.

Nelson, Vera M. *Siamese Cat Book.* Neptune, New Jersey: T.F.H. Publications, Inc., 1976.

BOOKS ABOUT RELATED BREEDS
Brearley, Joan McDonald. *All About Himalayan Cats.* Neptune, New Jersey: T.F.H. Publications, Inc., 1976.

Urcia, Ingeborg. *This Is The Rex.* Neptune, New Jersey: T.F.H. Publications, Inc., 1980.

Urcia, Ingeborg. *This Is The Russian Blue.* Neptune, New Jersey: T.F.H. Publications, Inc., 1980.

→

1. Sia Ti's Tai Tu by Ch. Sia Ti's Jaime x Sia Ti's Trinket, bred by Carol Morgart and owned by Debbie Thoms. The handsome Tai is a seven-year old Blue Point male. Often with Blues and Seals the characteristic point color spreads throughout the body as the cat matures. Many people find this most attractive and if you do too, be sure to find a breeder who raises this Siamese type before purchasing your new kitten. 2. Ch. Suzzi's Rembrandt of Velvet Paws, eight-year-old Chocolate male by Ch. Suzzi's Count Dragular x Suzzi's Never On Sunday; Mr. and Mrs. William A. Ramsden, Jr., breeders, Bill and Doris Thoms, owners. Rembrandt is an especially fine Siamese and has an exquisite head. Note that his point color has remained restricted to his extremities even though he is quite mature—this is characteristic of the Chocolates and Lilacs/Frosts in comparison to some of the Seals and Blues. Both photos by the author.

A floor-to-ceiling cat tree provides your pet with a place to climb, a scratching post and a perch from which to observe all that occurs in the room. Photo of "J.P." by Ruth Zimmermann.

GENERAL INTEREST TITLES

Browder, Sue. *The Pet Name Book*. New York: Workman Publishing Co., 1979.

Fogarty, Marna, ed. *The Cat Fancier's Association Yearbook*. Red Bank, New Jersey: CFA, Inc.

Gurney, Eric. *The Calculating Cat Returns*. Englewood Cliffs, New Jersey: Prentice-Hall, Inc., 1978.

Jude, A.C. *Cat Genetics*. New revised edition. Neptune, New Jersey: T.F.H. Publications, Inc., 1977.

Meins, Betty and Floyd, Wanita. *How To Show Your Cat*. Neptune, New Jersey: T.F.H. Publications, Inc., 1972.

Smythe, R.H. *Cat Psychology*. Neptune, New Jersey: T.F.H. Publications, Inc.

Wilson, Meredith. *Encyclopedia Of American Cat Breeds*. Neptune, New Jersey: T.F.H. Publications, Inc., 1978.

Wolfgang, Harriet. *Shorthaired Cats*. Neptune, New Jersey: T.F.H. Publications, Inc.

MAGAZINES

Siamese News Quarterly. 2588-C S. Vaughn Way, Aurora, Colorado 80014.

Cat Fancy. Monthly. 8322 Beverly Blvd., Los Angeles, California 90048.

Cat World. Bi-monthly. P.O. Box 597, Littleton, Colorado 80160.

Cats Mazagine. Monthly. P.O. Box 83048, Lincoln, Nebraska 68501.

Cat-Tab. Monthly. 7700 Old Dominion Drive, McLean, Virginia 22101.

Animals. Bi-monthly. 350 South Huntington Avenue, Boston, Massachusetts 02130.

My Pet. Quarterly. 160 Eglinton Avenue East, Suite 302, Toronto, Ontario, Canada M4P 1G3.

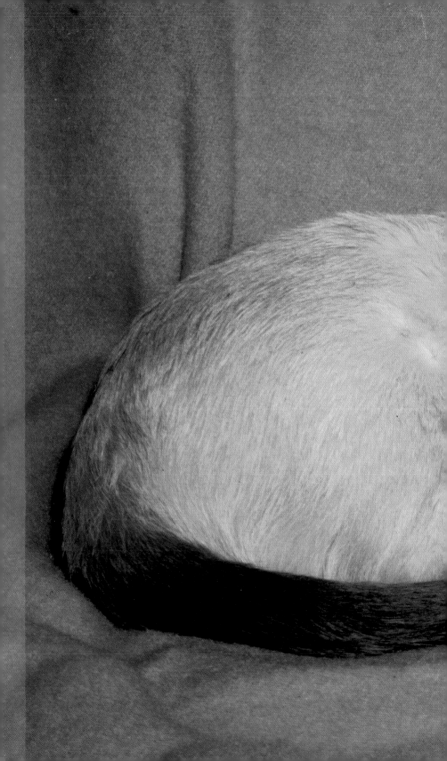